EMERIL LAGASSE
Everyday Recipes

Power
AirFryer 360™

ELPAF360_COOKBOOK_TP_ENG_V2_201009

Table of Contents

Breakfast & Baked Goods

Appetizers

Pizzas & Calzones

Burgers & Sandwiches

Entrées

Pork & Beef

Poultry

Seafood

Family-Style Dishes

Vegetables

Desserts

About
the Author

Emeril Lagasse is an Emmy-winning television personality, the chef and proprietor of 11 restaurants, a cookbook author, and a philanthropist. He is a James Beard Award winner known for his mastery of Creole and Cajun cuisine, which inspired the development of his "New New Orleans" style.

Chef Emeril is most notable for having appeared on a wide variety of cooking TV shows, including the long-running and highly rated Food Network shows Emeril Live and Essence of Emeril, and most recently, Amazon's original series Eat the World with Emeril Lagasse.

Chef Emeril believes that every home kitchen deserves appliances that offer a wide range of custom cooking capabilities. Designed for effortless one-touch cooking right on your countertop, the Power AirFryer 360 is a professional-quality multi-cooker that combines seamless air-flow with powerful, even heat.

EMERIL LAGASSE

E

EMERIL LAGASSE

Make delicious meals right on your countertop—from breakfast to dessert. Now, you can create Chef Emeril's recipes at home using the Emeril Lagasse Power AirFryer 360's state-of-the-art custom cooking capabilities. Let the results speak for themselves—you may find yourself imagining you're dining in one of Chef Emeril's award-winning restaurants.

Questions & Answers

1. What is the capacity?

The Emeril Lagasse Power AirFryer 360's inner capacity is 930 cubic in., which is large enough to accommodate a 12-in. round pizza or a 10-lb chicken.

2. Can I adjust the cooking time manually?

Yes! You can manually program the Emeril Lagasse Power AirFryer 360 to your chosen time and temperature. Alternatively, the Power AirFryer 360 has 12 one-touch pre-set functions.

3. Can I put frozen foods in the Emeril Lagasse Power AirFryer 360 without defrosting them first?

Yes! You do not have to allow frozen foods to thaw before cooking in the Power AirFryer 360.

4. Can I check my meals during the cooking process?

You can check the cooking process by pressing the Light Button or pressing the Start/Pause Button and then opening the door. You can press the Start/Pause Button again to resume the cooking cycle. Alternatively, you can press the Light Button to turn on the light inside the Emeril Lagasse Power AirFryer 360.

5. Is it possible to shut off the unit at any time?

Pressing the Cancel Button will stop the cooking cycle. Holding the Cancel Button for 3 seconds will turn off the Emeril Lagasse Power AirFryer 360.

6. Can I make more than one type of food at once?

Yes! The Emeril Lagasse Power AirFryer 360 is designed with multiple shelves that can be used with the included racks.

7. Can I make kabobs in the Emeril Lagasse Power AirFryer 360?

Yes! The Power AirFryer 360 is designed with a pro-grade rotisserie function. Rotisserie an entire chicken to tender, crisp perfection right in your own kitchen.

8. How do I dehydrate in the Emeril Lagasse Power AirFryer 360?

The Power AirFryer 360 is designed with a pro-grade, built-in dehydrator. You can easily dehydrate your favorite fresh meats, fruits, and veggies with no added sugar right at home on the included racks. See the Owner's Manual for specific instructions.

9. Do I have to use oil?

It is not necessary to use oil to air fry. The Emeril Lagasse Power AirFryer 360 cooks with super-heated air instead of oil. You may spray or coat your food with oil as desired for added flavor. Do not pour oil directly into the unit.

10. Do I need to preheat the Emeril Lagasse Power AirFryer 360?

The Power AirFryer 360 has a smart feature that will preheat the Unit to the set temperature before the timer begins counting down. This feature takes effect with all preprogrammed settings except Toast, Bagel, and Dehydrate.

11. Is the Emeril Lagasse Power AirFryer Oven 360 dishwasher safe?

The accessories are dishwasher safe. All other components may be washed with a small amount of nonabrasive soap and a nonmetallic sponge.

Why the Emeril Lagasse Power AirFryer 360?

Everyone loves fried food, but no one loves the extra calories that come with deep frying. With air frying, you can now fry your foods the healthy way—guilt free. Frying with air means you still get to enjoy all that great crispness and flavor without the extra fat and calories that come along with traditional frying in oil. Air frying gives you a lighter option than deep frying without sacrificing flavor.

The Emeril Lagasse Power AirFryer 360 improves the technology that made other air fryers like the Power AirFryer XL great by adding a rotisserie function, a professional-grade dehydrator, and more. The 9-in-1 Emeril Lagasse Power AirFryer 360 represents a new generation of all-purpose kitchen appliances. It is designed to replace traditional kitchen convection ovens, air fryers, and more with the cooking capabilities of a full-size unit. You get that beloved fried food taste and texture with up to 70% fewer calories from fat than traditional frying.

Best of all, the Emeril Lagasse Power AirFryer 360's one-touch technology lets you do it all at the touch of a button. Twelve one-touch presets let you get the perfect cooking results you want without all the hassle. Plus, the Emeril Lagasse Power AirFryer 360's extra-large capacity lets you cook meals for the whole family all at once.

Equivalency Charts

Dry (Weight) Measurements

Misc.*	Teaspoons	Tablespoons	Ounces	Cups	Grams	Pounds
1 dash	1/16 tsp.	-	-	-	-	-
1 pinch/6 drops	1/8 tsp.	-	-	-	-	-
15 drops	¼ tsp.	-	-	-	-	-
1 splash	½ tsp.	-	-	-	-	-
-	1 tsp.	1/3 tbsp.	1/6 oz	-	-	-
-	3 tsp.	1 tbsp.	½ oz	-	14.3 g	-
-	-	2 tbsp.	1 oz	1/8 cup	28.3 g	-
-	-	4 tbsp.	2 oz	¼ cup	56.7 g	-
-	-	5 1/3 tbsp.	2.6 oz	1/3 cup	75.6 g	-
-	-	8 tbsp.	4 oz	½ cup	113.4 g	-
-	-	12 tbsp.	6 oz	¾ cup	170.1 g	-
-	-	16 tbsp.	8 oz	1 cup	226.8 g	½ lb
-	-	32 tbsp.	16 oz	2 cups	453.6 g	1 lb
-	-	64 tbsp.	32 oz	4 cups/1 qt.	907.2 g	2 lb

* Dash, pinch, drop, and splash are subjective measurements that have no formally agreed-upon definition.

Abbreviations

Term	Dry & Liquid	Abbreviation
cup	usually liquid	-
fluid ounce	only liquid	fl oz.
gallon	dry or liquid	-
inch	-	in.
ounce	dry	oz.
pint	dry or liquid	-
pound	dry	lb
quart	dry or liquid	qt./qts.
teaspoon	dry or liquid	tsp.
tablespoon	dry or liquid	tbsp.

Liquid (Volume) Measurements

Fluid Ounces	Tablespoons	Cups	Milliliter/Liters	Pints	Quarts	Gallons
1 fl oz	2 tbsp.	⅛ cup	30 ml	-	-	-
2 fl oz	4 tbsp.	¼ cup	60 ml	-	-	-
4 fl oz	8 tbsp.	½ cup	125 ml	-	-	-
8 fl oz	16 tbsp.	1 cup	250 ml	-	-	-
12 fl oz	-	1 ½ cups	375 ml	-	-	-
16 fl oz	-	2 cups	500 ml	1 pint	-	-
32 fl oz	-	4 cups	1 L	2 pints	1 qt.	-
128 fl oz	-	16 cups	4 L	8 pints	4 qts.	1 gallon

Cooking Temperature Charts

Safe steps in food handling, cooking, and storage are essential for preventing foodborne illness. You can't see, smell, or taste harmful bacteria that may cause illness.

Cook all food to these minimum internal temperatures as measured with a food thermometer before removing food from the heat source. Let rest for a minimum of 10 mins. before serving unless indicated otherwise.

In every step of food preparation, follow the four guidelines to help keep food safe:

Clean—*Wash hands and surfaces often.*
Separate—*Separate raw meat from other foods.*
Cook—*Cook to the right temperature.*
Chill—*Refrigerate food promptly.*

Doneness	Serving Temperature	Serving Temperature
	Recommended	**USDA's Recommendation**
Pork Chops, Pork Loins & Pork Tenderloins		
Recommended	145° F (63° C)	*
Pork Ribs, Pork Shoulder, Pork Butt Roasts		
Recommended (Tender & Juicy)	190° F (88° C)	*
Beef, Lamb, Veal Steaks, Chops & Roasts		
Rare	125° F (52° C)	*
Medium Rare	130° F (54° C)	*
Medium	135° F (57° C)	
Medium Well	150° F (65° C)	Minimum Internal Temperature & Rest Time: 145° F (63° C) and allow to rest for at least 3 mins.*
Well Done	Over 150° F (over 65° C)	

Doneness	Serving Temperature	Serving Temperature
	Recommended	**USDA's Recommendation**
Ground Meats, Burgers, Meatloaf & Sausages Except Poultry		
Recommended	160° F (71° C)	Minimum Internal Temperature: 160° F (71° C)*
Burgers (Beef)		
Recommended	140° F (60° C)	160° F (71° C)
Precooked Ham		
Recommended	140° F (60° C)	Reheat cooked hams packaged in USDA-inspected plants to 140° F (60° C); all others to 165° F (74° C)*
Turkey & Chicken, Whole or Ground		
Recommended	165° F (74° C)	Minimum Internal Temperature: 165° F (74° C)*
Fish		
Rare	125° F (52° C)	*
Medium	135° F (57° C)	*
Well Done	145° F (63° C)	Minimum Internal Temperature: 145° F (63° C)*
Unpasteurized Eggs		
Recommended	160° F (71° C)	Minimum Internal Temperature: 160° F (71° C)*

*Consuming raw or undercooked meats, poultry, seafood, shellfish, or eggs may increase your risk of foodborne illness.
http://fsis.usda.gov/

Dehydration Chart

Food	Temperature	Time
Strawberry	125° F (52° C)	8–12 hrs.
Mango	125° F (52° C)	10 hrs.
Kiwi	125° F (52° C)	6 hrs.
Orange/Lemon	120° F (49° C)	12 hrs.
Pineapple	120°–125° F (49°–52° C)	10–12 hrs.
Watermelon	130° F (54° C)	30 hrs.
Papaya	120° F (49° C)	12 hrs.
Green Beans	125° F (52° C)	6 hrs.
Kale	125°–130° F (52°–54° C)	2–4 hrs.
Tomato	145° F (63° C)	10 hrs.
Beets	125° F (52° C)	10 hrs.
Cauliflower	130° F (54° C)	24 hrs.
Onion/Garlic	120° F (49° C)	10–12 hrs.
Parsley	125° F (52° C)	90 mins.
Rosemary	125° F (52° C)	2 hrs.
Thyme/Tarragon/Sage	125° F (52° C)	3 hrs.
Oregano	125° F (52° C)	2 hrs.
Chicken/Beef/Salmon	165° F (74° C)	5 hrs.

Note
- Do not leave the Power AirFryer 360 running unattended for an extended period.

Emeril's Accessories

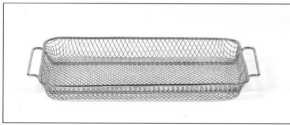

DRIP TRAY: Use to catch drippings from moist foods. Place in the bottom of the Unit just below the heating elements. Never use this Unit without the Drip Tray.

CRISPER TRAY: Use for cooking oil-free fried foods and broiling. Quantity may vary.

BAKING PAN: Use for baking and reheating various foods. Deeper oven-safe pans and dishes may be used in the Emeril Lagasse Power AirFryer 360.

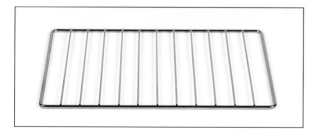

PIZZA RACK: Use for toasting breads, bagels, and pizzas; baking; grilling; and roasting. Quantity may vary.

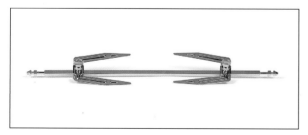

ROTISSERIE SPIT: Use for toasting breads, bagels, and pizzas; baking; grilling; and roasting. Quantity may vary.

Using the Accessories

AIR FRYING

STEP 1: Place food on a Crisper Tray and slide the Tray into Shelf Position 2. The Pizza Rack also slides into the shelves. The Baking Pan should be placed on top of the Pizza Rack when used. ***Always make sure the Drip Tray is in place.***

STEP 2: Use the Program Selection Knob to select the Airfry cooking preset.

STEP 3: Press the Start/Pause Button to begin the cooking process. You can press this button to pause during any cooking cycle.

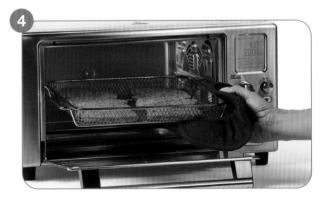

STEP 4: When the cooking cycle is complete, use oven mitts or potholders to remove the Crisper Tray from the Unit by sliding the Tray out of the Unit.

Notes

- Follow the air frying steps to use the Power AirFryer 360's Dehydration function. Simply adjust the cooking settings to dehydrate food. The Dehydrate function uses lower cooking temperatures and longer cooking times to dehydrate food.

- If you're cooking especially moist food in the Crisper Tray, you can place the Pizza Rack below the Crisper Tray and place the Baking Pan on the Pizza Rack to catch any drippings.

ROTISSERIE

STEP 1: Hold the Rotisserie Spit with the right side slightly higher than the left and insert the left side of the Spit into the connection inside the Unit. Then, drop the right side of the Spit into the other connection. ***Always make sure the Drip Tray is in place.***

STEP 2: Use the Program Selection Knob to select the Rotisserie cooking preset.

STEP 3: Press the Start/Pause Button to begin the cooking process. You can press this button to pause during any cooking cycle.

STEP 4: Use silicone oven mitts or use forks to pierce the meat and lift to remove the Rotisserie Spit by lifting the right side and then the left side of the Spit out of the connection points.

⚠ Caution

The Rotisserie parts are sharp, and all parts that rest inside the Emeril Lagasse Power AirFryer 360 during the cooking process become hot while the Unit is on. When you remove food or any of these parts during or after the cooking process, make sure you have a heat-resistant surface nearby on which to set the parts. NEVER place these parts directly on a table, countertop, or Oven door. Wear protective mitts or gloves when handling these parts to avoid injury.

Emeril's Seasonings

You can make these seasonings and store them in small **airtight containers**. These recipes **yield about ½–¾ cup**. Making extra seasonings saves time and money, and you will enjoy having some versatile flavors at the ready in your cooking arsenal. Keep a batch of the Creole seasoning on hand to give just about any savory dish a "kicked-up" flavor. The Baby Bam seasoning is great for those with a milder, less spicy palate. The Italian Essence is a no-sodium seasoning that can enhance many Italian-style dishes. See how many different things you can do with them!

Directions:

Place the ingredients in a mixing bowl and use a wooden spoon to stir together until well incorporated. Store in an airtight container for up to 3 months.

Baby Bam

3 tbsp. paprika

2 tbsp. salt

2 tbsp. dried parsley

2 tsp. onion powder

2 tsp. garlic powder

1 tsp. ground black pepper

1 tsp. dried oregano

1 tsp. dried basil

1 tsp. dried thyme

½ tsp. celery salt

Italian Essence

3 tbsp. dried oregano

3 tbsp. dried basil

2 tbsp. dried parsley

1 tbsp. dried rosemary, marjoram, or sage, rubbed between your fingers

1 tsp. crushed red pepper

2 tsp. onion powder

2 tsp. garlic powder

Creole Seasoning

2 ½ tbsp. paprika

2 tbsp. salt

2 tbsp. garlic powder

1 tbsp. black pepper

1 tbsp. onion powder

1 tbsp. cayenne pepper

1 tbsp. dried leaf oregano

1 tbsp. dried thyme

Breakfast & Baked Goods

Banana Bread

Zucchini Bread

Buttermilk Biscuits

Scallion & Cheddar Biscuits

Hash Brown Potatoes

Breakfast Strata with Italian Sausage & Bell Pepper

Quiche Lorraine

Broccoli & Cheddar Breakfast Soufflés

Shirred Eggs

One-Stop Breakfast Casserole

Lemon–Rosemary Buttermilk Scones

Strawberry Muffins

Granola with Dried Blueberries

EMERIL LAGASSE

Banana Bread

DIRECTIONS

1. Grease a standard-size loaf pan with 2 tsp. butter. Lightly dust the interior of the pan with flour and then tap out any excess flour. Reserve the prepared loaf pan.

2. Combine the banana with the light brown sugar and the rest of the butter in a medium-size bowl and use the back of a spoon to mash together.

3. Add the eggs, granulated sugar, vanilla extract, cinnamon, nutmeg, and salt to the bowl and whisk briskly to incorporate. Sift in the baking soda, baking powder, and ¾ cup flour and stir until just combined. Fold in the pecans and pour the batter into the prepared loaf pan.

4. Select the Bake setting (325° F/165° C). Set the cooking time to 40 mins. Press the Start Button to begin the cooking cycle. Let the Power AirFryer 360 preheat. Then, slide the Pizza Rack into Shelf Position 5. Place the loaf pan on the Pizza Rack. Cook until a wooden skewer or cake tester inserted into the banana bread's center comes out clean.

5. Remove the loaf pan from the Power AirFryer 360, invert the loaf, remove the pan, and turn the banana bread right side up. Slice and serve warm.

INGREDIENTS

½ cup plus 2 tsp. unsalted butter, softened, divided

1 ½ cups all-purpose flour, plus more for dusting a pan, divided

1 very ripe banana, peeled

½ cup light brown sugar

4 large eggs

½ cup granulated sugar

1 ½ tsp. vanilla extract

2 tsp. ground cinnamon

½ tsp. ground nutmeg

½ tsp. salt

½ tsp. baking soda

¼ tsp. baking powder

⅔ cup chopped pecans

Zucchini Bread

INGREDIENTS

4 large eggs

⅔ cup vegetable oil

1 cup sugar

1 cup grated unpeeled zucchini

2 tsp. vanilla extract

1 ½ cups all-purpose flour

1 tsp. ground cinnamon

½ tsp. baking soda

½ tsp. salt

¼ tsp. baking powder

½ cup lightly toasted
& chopped walnuts or pecans

cream cheese, room
temperature, for serving
(optional)

DIRECTIONS

1. Beat the eggs until foamy in a medium-size bowl. Add the vegetable oil, sugar, zucchini, and vanilla and mix well to incorporate. Add the flour, cinnamon, baking soda, salt, and baking powder and mix until well blended. Then, stir in the nuts. Pour the batter into a standard-size loaf pan and tap gently on the counter to release any air bubbles.

2. Slide the Pizza Rack into Shelf Position 5. Place the loaf pan on the Pizza Rack. Select the Bake setting (325° F/165° C for 30 mins.). Press the Start Button to begin the cooking cycle. Cook until the zucchini bread is cooked through and a toothpick inserted into its center comes out clean. If necessary, bake for an additional 5 mins.

3. Transfer the bread to a cooling rack for 5 mins. Then, invert the loaf, remove the pan, and turn the zucchini bread right side up.

4. Slice the bread and serve with the cream cheese spread on top if desired.

Buttermilk Biscuits

DIRECTIONS

1. Sift the all-purpose flour, cake flour, baking powder, baking soda, sugar, and salt into a medium-size bowl. Use your fingers or a pastry cutter to work the cubed butter into the flour until the pieces are pea sized. Add the buttermilk and use your hands or a rubber spatula to stir until the milk and flour come together to form a dough. Be careful not to overmix.

2. Lightly dust a work surface with flour. Turn the dough out onto the work surface. Use your hands to press the dough into a ½ in.-thick disk about 7–8 in. in diameter. Use a lightly floured 2 ½-in. round cutter to cut out six dough rounds. Be sure to press straight down when cutting the dough because a twisting motion will prevent the dough from rising.

3. Arrange the biscuits on the Crisper Tray. Brush them with 1 tbsp. melted butter. Slide the Crisper Tray into Shelf Position 5. Select the Airfry setting (400° F/205° C). Set the cooking time to 8 mins. Press the Start Button to begin the cooking cycle.

4. Serve the biscuits with the butter, preserves, or honey.

INGREDIENTS

1 ¼ cups all-purpose flour, plus more for dusting

½ cup cake flour

½ tsp. baking powder

¼ tsp. baking soda

1 tsp. granulated sugar

¾ tsp. salt

¼ cup unsalted butter, cold & cut into cubes

1 tbsp. butter, melted

¾ cup buttermilk

butter, softened, for serving (optional)

fruit preserves, for serving (optional)

honey, for serving (optional)

Scallion & Cheddar Biscuits

MAKES 6

DIRECTIONS

1. Sift the all-purpose flour, cake flour, baking powder, baking soda, sugar, and salt into a medium-size bowl. Use your fingers or a pastry cutter to work the cubed butter into the flour until the pieces are pea sized.

2. Add the cheddar and scallions and toss to combine. Add the buttermilk and use your hands or a rubber spatula to stir until the milk and flour come together to form a dough. Be careful not to overmix.

3. Lightly dust a work surface with flour. Turn the dough out onto the work surface. Use your hands to press the dough into a ½ in.-thick disk about 8 in. in diameter. Use a lightly floured 2 ½-in. round cutter to cut out six dough rounds. Be sure to press straight down when cutting the dough because a twisting motion will prevent the dough from rising.

4. Lightly brush the Baking Pan with a bit of the melted butter. Then, arrange the biscuits in a single layer on the Baking Pan and brush the biscuits with 1 tbsp. melted butter.

5. Slide the Pizza Rack into Shelf Position 5. Place the Baking Pan on top of the Pizza Rack. Select the Airfry setting (400° F/205° C). Set the cooking time to 8 mins. Press the Start Button to begin the cooking cycle. Cook until the biscuits are golden brown.

6. Serve with the softened butter.

INGREDIENTS

1 ¼ cups all-purpose flour, plus more for dusting

½ cup cake flour

¾ tsp. baking powder

¼ tsp. baking soda

1 tsp. granulated sugar

¾ tsp. salt

¼ cup unsalted butter, cold & cut into cubes

½ cup grated cheddar

3 tbsp. chopped scallions

¾ cup plus 2 tbsp. buttermilk

3 tbsp. butter, melted

softened butter, for serving

Hash Brown Potatoes

INGREDIENTS

3 tbsp. vegetable oil

1 ½ cups chopped onions

½ cup chopped red bell peppers

½ cup chopped green bell peppers

1 tbsp. minced garlic

1 tbsp. fresh thyme leaves

1 tsp. salt

½ tsp. black pepper

4 cups frozen shredded potatoes

DIRECTIONS

1. Combine all the ingredients in a bowl and toss.

2. Place the potatoes on the Baking Pan.

3. Slide the Pizza Rack into Shelf Position 1. Place the Baking Pan on top of the Pizza Rack. Select the Airfry setting (400° F/205° C). Set the cooking time to 45 mins. Press the Start Button to begin the cooking cycle. Stir the potatoes every 10 mins. while they are cooking.

4. Serve the hash browns with eggs.

Breakfast Strata
with Italian Sausage & Bell Pepper

DIRECTIONS

1. Place the bell peppers and onion strips on the Baking Pan and top them with the sausage. Cover the Baking Pan with foil.

2. Slide the Pizza Rack into Shelf Position 1. Place the Baking Pan on top of the Pizza Rack. Select the Bake setting (325° F/165° C for 30 mins.). Press the Start Button to begin the cooking cycle.

3. When the cooking time is complete, remove the foil. Select the Airfry setting (400° F/205° C). Set the cooking time to 5 mins. Press the Start Button to begin the cooking cycle.

4. While the sausage and veggies are cooking, combine the eggs, half and half, ground cayenne pepper, salt, and herbs in a bowl and whisk. Add the bread cubes and stir. Allow the bread to sit for at least 10 mins.

5. When the cooking time is complete, butter a 2-qt. casserole dish with 1 tbsp. butter. Transfer half of the vegetable–sausage mixture from the Baking Pan to the casserole dish. Spoon half of the bread mixture over the vegetable–sausage mixture and then top with half of the Fontina and Parmesan. Spoon the reserved vegetable–sausage mixture over the cheese and then top with the rest of the bread mixture and the rest of the cheese. Cover the casserole dish tightly with a piece of buttered aluminum foil (buttered side down).

6. Slide the Pizza Rack into Shelf Position 5. Place the casserole dish on the Pizza Rack. Select the Bake setting (325° F/165° C for 30 mins.). Press the Start Button to begin the cooking cycle.

7. When the cooking time is complete, Select the Airfry setting (400° F/205° C). Set the cooking time to 5 mins. Press the Start Button to begin the cooking cycle.

8. Let rest for at least 10 mins. before serving.

INGREDIENTS

½ red bell pepper, cut into ½-in. strips lengthwise

½ green bell pepper, cut into ½-in. strips lengthwise

½ medium-size onion, cut into ½-in. strips lengthwise

10 oz mild Italian sausage, removed from casings & broken into bite-size pieces

5 large eggs

1 ½ cups half and half

¼ tsp. plus 1 pinch ground cayenne pepper

¾ tsp. kosher salt

1 ½ tbsp. chopped fresh herbs, such as oregano, basil & marjoram

5 cups 1-in. cubed seeded Italian bread

1 tbsp. butter

4 oz grated Fontina

¼ cup finely grated Parmesan

Quiche Lorraine

DIRECTIONS

1. Lightly dust a work surface with flour. Turn the dough out onto the work surface. Invert a 10-in. plate on top of the pie dough and, using the plate as a template, cut around the dough's edges to make a pie shell. Discard the rest of the dough and lay the formed dough into a 9-in. pie pan, easing the dough into the bottom of the pan so that the dough fits snugly against all edges.

2. Fold the edges of the dough under itself so that the folded edges sit above the rim of the pie pan. Crimp the edges of the pie dough to form a decorative edge. Line the dough using parchment paper and add pie weights or beans to weight the shell.

3. Slide the Pizza Rack into Shelf Position 5. Place the pie pan on the Pizza Rack. Select the Airfry setting (400° F/205° C). Set the cooking time to 10 mins. Press the Start Button to begin the cooking cycle.

4. When the cooking time is complete, remove the foil and pie weights from the pie shell. Return the pie pan to the Power AirFryer 360.

5. Select the Airfry setting (400° F/205° C). Set the cooking time to 2 mins. Press the Start Button to begin the cooking cycle. Cook until the bottom of the crust is lightly golden. Then, open the Power AirFryer 360 and let the crust cool.

6. Place a small sauté pan on the stove top. Melt the butter over medium heat. Then, add the mushrooms and onions and cook while stirring often until the mushrooms and onions are softened (4–6 mins.)

7. Add the ham, cook briefly, and remove the sauté pan from the heat. Add the mixture to the baked pie shell.

8. Add the egg, egg yolk, cream, salt, black pepper, nutmeg, and thyme to a medium-size mixing bowl and whisk until well blended. Carefully pour the mixture into the pie crust on top of the vegetables and ham. Sprinkle the cheese over the mixture.

9. Return the pie pan to the Power AirFryer 360. Select the Bake setting. Set the cooking temperature to 300° F/149° C and set the cooking time to 25 mins. Press the Start Button to begin the cooking cycle. Cook until the crust is golden brown and the quiche is set.

10. Let the quiche cool for 20 mins. before cutting into wedges.

INGREDIENTS

all-purpose flour, for dusting

1 store-bought or homemade prepared pie dough, room temperature

1 tbsp. unsalted butter

2 oz button mushrooms (about 4 mushrooms), chopped

½ cup small-diced yellow onions

¼ cup diced ham

1 large egg

1 egg yolk

¾ cup heavy cream

¼ tsp. salt

¼ tsp. ground black pepper

⅛ tsp. ground nutmeg

½ tsp. fresh thyme

½ cup grated Gruyère, Jarlsberg, or Swiss cheese

Broccoli & Cheddar

Breakfast Soufflés

DIRECTIONS

1. Combine the eggs, garlic, cottage cheese, salt, and ground cayenne pepper in a blender and process until smooth and creamy.

2. Pour the mixture into a large mixing bowl. Add the broccoli, cheddar, and scallions and stir to combine. Then, ladle the mixture into six greased ½-cup ramekins.

3. Slide the Pizza Rack into Shelf Position 5. Place the ramekins on the Pizza Rack. Select the Bake setting. Set the cooking temperature to 300° F/149° C and set the cooking time to 22 mins. Press the Start Button to begin the cooking cycle. Cook until the soufflés are puffed and golden brown on top.

4. Serve with salad.

INGREDIENTS

5 large eggs

1 clove garlic

¾ cup low-fat cottage cheese

½ tsp. salt

¼ plus ⅛ tsp. ground cayenne pepper

2 cups finely chopped broccoli

¾ cup shredded cheddar

3 tbsp. thinly sliced scallions

salad, for serving

Shirred Eggs

INGREDIENTS

2 tsp. unsalted butter, softened

4 thin slices Black Forest ham (about 1 ½–2 oz total)

4 large eggs

4 tbsp. heavy cream

¾ tsp. kosher salt

¼ tsp. ground black pepper

4 tbsp. finely grated Parmesan

⅛ tsp. pimentón or paprika, for sprinkling

4 tsp. chopped fresh chives

toasted bread, for serving (optional)

DIRECTIONS

1. Butter four 6-oz ramekins and lay 1 slice of ham at the bottom of each ramekin.

2. Crack 1 egg into each ramekin. Drizzle 1 tbsp. heavy cream over each egg. Season the eggs with the salt and black pepper and sprinkle the Parmesan over each egg.

3. Slide the Pizza Rack into Shelf Position 5. Place the Baking Pan on the Pizza Rack. Place the ramekins on the Baking Pan. Select the Bake setting (325° F/165° C). Set the cooking time to 10 mins. Press the Start Button to begin the cooking cycle.

4. When the cooking time is complete, remove the ramekins and garnish with the pimentón and chives. Serve with the toasted bread if desired.

One-Stop Breakfast Casserole

DIRECTIONS

1. Place a skillet on the stove top. Heat the skillet over medium heat. Then, add the sausage and cook the sausage while breaking it into small pieces with a wooden spoon until the sausage begins to brown (about 4 mins.).

2. Add the shallots to the skillet and cook until the meat is golden brown and the shallots are soft (about 2 mins.). Then, remove the skillet from the heat.

3. Butter a 9 x 9 3-qt. casserole dish and line the bottom of the dish with half of the bread slices. Top the bread slices with half of the sausage–shallot mixture and half of the grated Monterey Jack. Make another layer with the remaining bread, sausage, and Monterey Jack.

4. Combine the eggs, half and half, salt, and black pepper in a mixing bowl and whisk to combine.

5. Pour the egg mixture evenly over the layered bread mixture. Cover with plastic wrap and refrigerate for at least 1 hr. (up to overnight).

6. Remove the casserole from the refrigerator and allow it to come to room temperature for about 20 mins.

7. Slide the Pizza Rack into Shelf Position 6. Place the baking dish on the Pizza Rack. Select the Bake setting (30-min. cooking time). Set the cooking temperature to 325° F/163° C. Press the Start Button to begin the cooking cycle. Cook until the casserole is set.

INGREDIENTS

8 oz breakfast sausage, casings removed

2 large shallots, minced

1 tbsp. butter

12–16 ½ in.-thick slices day-old French bread

6 oz shredded Monterey Jack

10 large eggs

2 ½ cups half and half

½ tsp. salt

¼ tsp. ground white pepper

Lemon–Rosemary Buttermilk Scones

DIRECTIONS

1. Sift together the flour, sugar, baking powder, baking soda, salt, and black pepper in a medium-size bowl. Add the lemon zest and rosemary and combine with a fork. Use a fork, your fingers, or a pastry blender to work the butter into the flour until the mixture resembles coarse crumbs.

2. Add ½ cup plus 1 tbsp. buttermilk and stir with a fork until the ingredients are just moistened. Gather the dough together and press it gently into a rough ball. Turn the dough out onto a lightly floured surface, flour your hands, and pat the dough together. The dough may still be crumbly. Knead the dough gently until it just comes together and then shape it into a rectangle shape. Use a lightly floured rolling pin to roll the dough to a thickness of about ¾ in. Cut the dough crosswise into three portions and then cut each portion into two triangle shapes. You should have six generously sized scones.

3. Select the Airfry setting (400° F/205° C). Set the cooking time to 14 mins. Press the Start Button to begin the cooking cycle. Let the Power AirFryer 360 preheat.

4. Cut parchment paper to match the size of the Crisper Tray and Baking Pan. Line the Crisper Tray and Baking Pan with the parchment paper. Place the scones on the Crisper Tray and Baking Pan. Brush the tops of the scones lightly with the rest of the buttermilk.

5. Slide the Pizza Rack into Shelf Position 1. Place the Baking Pan on top of the Pizza Rack. Slide the Crisper Tray into Shelf Position 2. Halfway through the cooking time (7 mins.), slide the Crisper Tray into Shelf Position 5 and slide the Baking Pan/Pizza Rack into Shelf Position 2.

6. Serve with the butter, lemon curd, jam, or clotted cream.

INGREDIENTS

1 ½ cups all-purpose flour

2 tsp. sugar

1 ½ tsp. baking powder

¼ tsp. baking soda

½ tsp. salt

⅛ tsp. freshly ground black pepper

½ tsp. finely grated lemon zest

1 ½ tsp. finely chopped fresh rosemary

¼ cup plus 2 tbsp. unsalted butter, cold & cut into pieces

½ cup plus 2 tbsp. well-shaken buttermilk, divided

butter, softened, for serving (optional)

lemon curd, for serving (optional)

clotted cream, for serving (optional)

Strawberry Muffins

DIRECTIONS

1. Place the strawberries in a blender or food processor and purée on high speed.

2. Beat together the eggs, sugar, and vegetable oil in a large bowl. Then, add the strawberries and whisk until well blended.

3. Sift together the flour, baking soda, baking powder, cinnamon, and salt in a separate bowl.

4. Fold the dry ingredients into the strawberry mixture, blending until moistened. Then, fold in the macadamia nuts. Be careful not to overmix.

5. Pour a scant ½ cup batter into twelve standalone muffin cups.

6. Select the Bake setting (325° F/165° C). Set the cooking time to 20 mins. Press the Start Button to begin the cooking cycle. Allow the Power AirFryer 360 to preheat.

7. When the Power AirFryer 360 has preheated, place six muffin cups on the Crisper Tray. Slide the Crisper Tray into Shelf Position 5. Cook until a tester inserted into the muffins comes out clean and the muffins are lightly browned around the edges. When the first batch of muffins is done cooking, repeat the cooking process with the rest of the muffins.

INGREDIENTS

2 cups sliced & hulled strawberries

2 large eggs

1 cup sugar

½ cup vegetable oil

1 ½ cups all-purpose flour

1 tsp. baking soda

½ tsp. baking powder

½ tsp. ground cinnamon

¼ tsp. salt

½ cup toasted & chopped macadamia nuts

Granola with Dried Blueberries

DIRECTIONS

Dehydrated Blueberries:

1. Place the blueberries on the Crisper Tray. Slide the Crisper Tray into Shelf Position 2.

2. Select the Dehydrate setting. Set the cooking temperature to 120° F/49° C and set the cooking time to 20 hrs. Press the Start Button to begin the cooking cycle.

Granola:

1. Combine the granola ingredients in a bowl and mix.

2. Spread the granola on the Baking Pan. Slide the Pizza Rack into Shelf Position 1. Place the Baking Pan on top of the Pizza Rack. Select the Bake setting (30-min. cooking time). Set the cooking temperature to 300° F/149° C. Press the Start Button to begin the cooking cycle. Halfway through the cooking time (15 mins.), stir the granola.

3. When the cooking time is complete, remove the granola, let cool, and mix with the dried blueberries.

4. Serve with yogurt.

INGREDIENTS

Dehydrated Blueberries

4 cups blueberries, rinsed

Granola

2 cups oats

½ cup sunflower seeds, walnuts & almonds

½ cup brown sugar

1 tsp. cinnamon

1 tsp. nutmeg

4 tbsp. wheat germ

6 tbsp. butter, melted

1 tbsp. vanilla extract

Appetizers

Cocktail Meatballs

Bean & Cheese Quesadillas

Chicken Wings with a Lemon
& Honey Drizzle

Viet-Style Curry Chicken Wings

Chinese-Style Shrimp Toast

Pigs in a Blanket with Mustard
Dipping Sauce

Shrimp & Pork Vietnamese Egg Rolls

Beef Jerky

Ham Hock & Lentil Soup

Orange-Flavored Brandy

Kicked-Up Jalapeño Poppers

Cheese-Stuffed Mushrooms

Spanakopita

Crab Rangoons

Baked Brie with Pistachios & Apricots

EMERIL LAGASSE

Cocktail Meatballs

DIRECTIONS

1. Combine the meatball ingredients in a bowl. Divide the mixture into 1-in. balls.

2. Place the meatballs on the Crisper Tray. Slide the Crisper Tray into Shelf Position 2. Select the Airfry setting (400° F/205° C). Set the cooking time to 10 mins. Press the Start Button to begin the cooking cycle.

3. While the meatballs cook, combine the sauce ingredients in a medium-size bowl and whisk to dissolve the sugar.

4. When the cooking time is complete, transfer the meatballs to a 4 ½-qt. casserole dish and pour the sauce over the meatballs. Cover the dish with its lid or, if necessary, aluminum foil.

5. Slide the Pizza Rack into Shelf Position 6. Place the dish on the Rack. Select the Bake setting (325° F/165° C for 30 mins.). Press the Start Button to begin the cooking cycle.

6. When the cooking time is complete, carefully remove the dish and serve the meatballs.

INGREDIENTS

Meatballs

1 lb ground beef

1 large egg, beaten lightly

½ cup finely chopped yellow onion

¼ cup fine dry breadcrumbs

2 tbsp. grated Parmesan

2 tbsp. milk

2 tsp. Creole mustard

1 ½ tsp. minced garlic

½ tsp. dried basil

½ tsp. dried oregano

½ tsp. dried parsley

½ tsp. Creole seasoning (see p. 25)

½ tsp. salt

¼ tsp. ground black pepper

½ tsp. Worcestershire sauce

¼ tsp. hot red pepper sauce

2 tsp. vegetable oil

2 tsp. unsalted butter

Sauce

1 cup ketchup

½ cup grated yellow onions

1 tsp. minced garlic

¼ cup packed light brown sugar

¼ cup red wine vinegar

1 tbsp. Worcestershire sauce

¼ tsp. ground black pepper

1 tsp. salt

Bean & Cheese Quesadillas

SERVES 4

INGREDIENTS

¼ cup olive oil

½ yellow onion, thinly sliced

¼ red bell pepper, thinly sliced

¼ green bell pepper, thinly sliced

1 clove garlic, minced

½ tsp. ground coriander

½ tsp. ground cumin

½ tsp. salt

¼ tsp. ground cayenne pepper

¼ tsp. chili powder

8 6-in. flour tortillas

¾ cup grated pepper jack

¾ cup pinto beans, drained & slightly smashed

salsa, for garnish

guacamole, for garnish

sour cream, for garnish

DIRECTIONS

1. Place a medium-size sauté pan on the stove top. Add the olive oil and heat the oil over medium heat. When the oil is hot, add the onion, bell peppers, and garlic and cook while stirring for 3 mins.

2. Add the coriander, cumin, salt, ground cayenne pepper, and chili powder and continue to cook until the onion and peppers are soft (about 3 mins.). Then, remove the sauté pan from the heat.

3. Lay the tortillas on a clean work surface. Sprinkle each tortilla with 1 ½ tbsp. pepper jack, 1 ½ tbsp. beans, and 2 tbsp. pepper mixture. Sandwich the tortillas together and brush each side with the rest of the olive oil.

4. Place two quesadillas on the Crisper Tray and two on the Pizza Rack. Slide the Pizza Rack into Shelf Position 6. Slide the Crisper Tray into Shelf Position 1. Select the Bake setting. Set the cooking temperature to 350° F/177° C and set the cooking time to 10 mins. Press the Start Button to begin the cooking cycle. Halfway through the cooking time (5 mins.), slide the Crisper Tray into Shelf Position 5 and slide the Pizza Rack into Shelf Position 1. Cook until the tortillas are golden brown and the cheese has melted.

5. When the quesadillas are done cooking, carefully transfer them to a cutting board and cut them into four portions. Serve with the guacamole, salsa, and sour cream.

Chicken Wings

with a Lemon & Honey Drizzle

DIRECTIONS

1. Combine the chicken, pimentón, salt, and ground cayenne pepper in a medium-size bowl and toss well to combine. Drizzle the olive oil over the chicken and toss to coat.

2. Place the chicken in the Crisper Tray. Slide the Crisper Tray into Shelf Position 2. Select the Airfry setting (400° F/205° C). Set the cooking time to 40 mins. Press the Start Button to begin the cooking cycle. Turn the chicken every 10 mins. while it is cooking to promote even browning. Cook until the internal temperature of the chicken reaches 165° F/74° C and the chicken is nicely browned.

3. While the chicken cooks, combine the honey, lemon juice, and black pepper in a small bowl and stir to combine.

4. When the cooking time is complete, transfer the chicken to a bowl, toss the chicken with the honey–lemon drizzle, and serve immediately.

INGREDIENTS

2 ½ lb chicken wings, separated at joints & wing tips removed

1 tbsp. pimentón

1 ½ tsp. kosher salt

½ tsp. ground cayenne pepper

1 tbsp. olive oil

¼ cup honey

1 ½ tbsp. freshly squeezed lemon juice

1 tsp. coarsely ground black pepper

Viet-Style Curry Chicken Wings

DIRECTIONS

1. Place all the ingredients except the cilantro in a large resealable plastic bag. Close the bag and use your hands to move the chicken around to evenly distribute the spices in the marinade. Refrigerate for at least 4 hrs. (up to overnight).

2. Remove the chicken from the refrigerator and let sit for 30 mins. to reach room temperature.

3. Place the chicken on the Crisper Tray. Slide the Crisper Tray into Shelf Position 2. Select the Airfry setting (400° F/205° C). Set the cooking time to 40 mins. Press the Start Button to begin the cooking cycle. Cook while turning the chicken every 10 mins. to promote even browning until the internal temperature of the chicken reaches 165° F/74° C and the wings are nicely browned.

4. When the chicken is done cooking, let it cool briefly before serving. Garnish the chicken with the cilantro.

INGREDIENTS

2 ¼–2 ½ lb chicken wings, separated at the joints & wing tips discarded

¾ tsp. kosher salt

2 tsp. sugar

1 tbsp. Madras curry powder

1 tbsp. Vietnamese fish sauce

2 tbsp. canola or grapeseed oil

1 large shallot, minced

2 Thai chiles, minced (with seeds)

2 stalks lemongrass, inner bulb chopped finely

1 tsp. minced garlic

2 tbsp. chopped fresh cilantro, for garnish

Chinese-Style Shrimp Toast

INGREDIENTS

2 cloves garlic, chopped roughly

1 egg white

1 tbsp. rice wine

1 tbsp. cornstarch

1 tbsp. soy sauce

2 tsp. minced ginger

1 ½ tsp. chile garlic sauce

1 tsp. sugar

1 lb shrimp, peeled & deveined

12 very thin slices white sandwich bread, crusts discarded

¼ cup toasted sesame seeds

DIRECTIONS

1. Combine the garlic, egg white, rice wine, cornstarch, soy sauce, ginger, chile garlic sauce, and sugar in a food processor and blend well. Add the shrimp in batches and pulse to blend to a rough paste. Then, transfer the shrimp spread to a small bowl.

2. Divide the shrimp spread among the bread slices (about 1 heaping tbsp. per slice). Spread evenly to cover the whole bread slice. Dredge each slice in the sesame seeds and coat well. Cut each bread slice in half diagonally to form triangles.

3. Evenly divide the shrimp toast on the Crisper Tray and Baking Pan. Slide the Pizza Rack into Shelf Position 1. Place the Baking Pan on top of the Pizza Rack. Slide the Crisper Tray into Shelf Position 2.

4. Select the Airfry setting (400° F/205° C). Set the cooking time to 10 mins. Press the Start Button to begin the cooking cycle. Halfway through the cooking time (5 mins.), slide the Tray into Shelf Position 5 and slide the Baking Pan/Pizza Rack into Shelf Position 2. Cook until lightly golden.

5. Serve warm.

Pigs in a Blanket
with Mustard Dipping Sauce

DIRECTIONS

1. Lightly dust a work surface with flour. Roll out the puff pastry sheet until ⅛ in. thick and cut the sheet into 1 ½-in. squares.

2. Wrap each cocktail sausage in a square of the pastry, bringing two opposite corners together over the middle of the sausage. Brush the inside of one of the corners with a bit of the beaten egg and overlap the corners, pressing to seal the edges over the sausage. Repeat until each sausage has been wrapped in pastry.

3. Evenly divide the sausage between the Crisper Tray and Baking Pan. Slide the Pizza Rack into Shelf Position 1. Place the Baking Pan on top of the Pizza Rack. Slide the Crisper Tray into Shelf Position 2. Select the Airfry setting. Set the cooking temperature to 370° F/188° C and set the cooking time to 7 mins. Press the Start Button to begin the cooking cycle. Cook until the pastry is golden brown and puffed.

4. While the sausages are cooking, place a small saucepan on the stove top. Combine the jelly, mustard, and butter in the saucepan and cook while whisking over low heat until the jelly and butter melt into the mustard and the mixture is smooth.

5. Transfer the sauce to a bowl and serve the pigs in a blanket with the sauce.

INGREDIENTS

flour, for dusting a work surface

1 sheet puff pastry, thawed according to package directions

1 12-oz package smoked cocktail sausages, patted dry

1 egg, beaten

5 oz guava jelly

¼ cup plus 2 tbsp. Dijon or country Dijon mustard

¼ cup butter

Shrimp & Pork Vietnamese Egg Rolls

SERVES 12

DIRECTIONS

1. Combine the sugar and warm water in a bowl and let the sugar dissolve. Combine the lime juice, fish sauce, and Thai chile to make the nuoc cham. Reserve the nuoc cham.

2. Place a wok or large sauté pan on the stove top. Heat the vegetable oil over medium-high heat. When the oil is hot, add the sausage and stir fry for 3 mins. Then, add the yellow onion and garlic and cook for 2 mins. Finally, add the bok choy and shrimp and stir fry for 1 min.

3. Season with the chile garlic sauce and 3 tbsp. nuoc cham. Reserve the rest of the nuoc cham.

4. Remove the wok/sauté pan from the heat and let cool completely. Then, stir in the scallion.

5. Combine the bean sprouts, carrots, cilantro, and mint and dress lightly with the nuoc cham. Reserve the salad and the rest of the nuoc cham.

6. Spread 2 tbsp. shrimp mixture in the bottom quarter of each spring roll wrapper. Fold two sides of the wrapper toward the center and then roll like a jelly roll, pressing the edges together to seal. Repeat until all 24 rolls are sealed. Brush the egg rolls with canola oil.

7. Evenly divide the egg rolls between the Crisper Tray and Baking Pan. Slide the Pizza Rack into Shelf Position 1. Place the Baking Pan on top of the Pizza Rack. Slide the Crisper Tray into Shelf Position 2. Select the Airfry setting. Set the cooking temperature to 380° F/193° C and set the cooking time to 7 mins. Press the Start Button to begin the cooking cycle.

8. When the cooking time is complete, remove the egg rolls and drain them on paper towels. Repeat until all the egg rolls are cooked.

9. Serve with the nuoc cham (for dipping) and the carrot and herb salad.

INGREDIENTS

Nuoc Cham

3 tbsp. sugar

½ cup water, warm

⅓ cup lime juice

2 tbsp. fish sauce

1 Thai chile, chopped finely

_____

2 tbsp. vegetable oil

½ lb Chinese sausage, chopped finely

½ cup minced yellow onion

1 tbsp. chopped garlic

¼ lb bok choy, shredded

½ lb medium shrimp, peeled, deveined & chopped

1 tbsp. chile garlic sauce

1 tbsp. chopped scallions

1 cup bean sprouts

1 cup matchstick carrot strips

1 cup packed cilantro leaves

1 cup packed fresh mint leaves

24 spring roll wrappers

canola oil, for brushing

Beef Jerky

INGREDIENTS

2 lb beef or buffalo sirloin, trimmed of fat & sinew

4 tbsp. soy sauce

3 tbsp. brown sugar

4 cloves garlic, peeled & smashed

2 tbsp. Worcestershire sauce

1 tbsp. liquid smoke

2 tsp. red pepper flakes

2 tsp. onion powder

2 tsp. chili powder

1 tsp. salt

1 tsp. freshly ground black pepper

DIRECTIONS

1. Slice the meat into strips against the grain ¼ in. thick and 1 in. wide (if necessary, freeze the meat for up to 2 hrs. beforehand to facilitate slicing).

2. Combine the soy sauce, brown sugar, garlic, Worcestershire sauce, liquid smoke, red pepper flakes, onion powder, chili powder, salt, and black pepper in a large, wide bowl. Place the meat in the marinade, cover the bowl, and marinate the meat in the refrigerator overnight, turning occasionally.

3. Drain the meat, pat it dry, and arrange it evenly on the Pizza Rack and the Crisper Tray. Slide the Pizza Rack into Shelf Position 6. Slide the Crisper Tray into Shelf Position 2.

4. Select the Dehydrate setting. Set the cooking temperature to 145° F/63° C and set the cooking time to 12 hrs. Press the Start Button to begin the cooking cycle. Turn the meat once or twice while cooking and cook until the meat is dry but still firm (not spongy or brittle).

5. When the beef jerky is done, remove it from the oven and store it in wax paper at room temperature for up to 2 days. Alternatively, wrap the jerky in plastic and refrigerate to store for up to 1 week.

Ham Hock & Lentil Soup

DIRECTIONS

Soup Mirepoix:*

1. Line the Pizza Rack with parchment paper. Place the celery slices and carrot slices in a single layer on the Crisper Tray. Place the onion slices in a single layer on the Pizza Rack.

2. Slide the Tray into Shelf Position 2. Slide the Rack into Shelf Position 5. Set the Power AirFryer 360 to the Dehydrate setting (125° F/52° C) and set the cooking time to 12 hrs. Press the Start/Pause Button to begin the cooking cycle.

Ham Hock & Lentil Soup:

1. Place a large 6-qt. pot on the stove top. Heat the olive oil over medium heat. When the oil is hot, add the soup mirepoix, season with the salt and black pepper, and sauté for 2 mins.

2. Add the garlic, bay leaves and thyme and sauté for 1 min.

3. Add the ham hocks and stock. Bring the liquid to a boil and then reduce the heat to medium-low. Cook, covered until the hocks are tender (about 1 hr.).

4. Remove the lid, add the lentils, continue cook, stirring as needed until the lentils are tender (25–30 mins.). Remove from the heat and stir in the parsley. Season with salt and black pepper if needed.

5. Remove the ham hocks and remove the meat from the skin and bone. Then, add the ham back into the soup.

6. Ladle the soup into individual bowls and serve with crusty bread.

* Dehydrating soup mirepoix can be a great way of preserving celery, carrots, or onions before they expire. One great use for mirepoix is camping: Just add water to rehydrate the vegetables.

INGREDIENTS

Soup Mirepoix

1 stalks celery, sliced into ¼-in. pieces

1 carrot, peeled & sliced into ¼-in. medallions

1 large white onion, peeled & thinly sliced

Ham Hock & Lentil Soup

2 tbsp. olive oil

¼ cup soup mirepoix (refer to recipe)

salt, for seasoning

freshly ground black pepper, for seasoning

2 tbsp. chopped garlic

2 bay leaves

6 sprigs of fresh thyme

3–4 smoked ham hocks

2 qts. chicken stock

1 lb orange lentils

2 tbsp. chopped parsley

Orange-Flavored Brandy

DIRECTIONS

Dehydrated Oranges:

1. Slide the Crisper Tray into Shelf Position 2. Slide the Pizza Rack into Shelf Position 2. Place the sliced oranges on the Crisper Tray and Pizza Rack.

2. Select the Dehydrate setting (120° F/49° C). Set the cooking time to 12 hrs. Press the Start Button to begin the cooking cycle.

Brandy:

1. Place the oranges in a jar or bottle. Pour the brandy over the oranges and let sit overnight.

2. After sitting overnight, place five snifters on the countertop. Pour 2 oz brandy into each snifter.

3. Garnish with orange slices.

INGREDIENTS

Dehydrated Oranges

2 oranges, sliced ¼ in. thick

Brandy

12 slices dehydrated oranges, plus more for garnish

10 oz brandy

Kicked-Up Jalapeño Poppers

DIRECTIONS

1. Cut a slit lengthwise down one side of each jalapeño to create a pocket, leaving the stem intact. Use a paring knife or small spoon to carefully scrape the inside of the jalapeños to remove some of the seeds to make room for the filling.

2. Combine the cream cheese, Monterey Jack, bacon, and ½ tsp. Creole seasoning in a small bowl. Place the mixture in a large piping bag or a resealable plastic food storage bag (if using a food storage bag, cut one corner of the bag to form a hole large enough to allow the bacon pieces to squeeze through).

3. Squeeze the mixture to the bottom of the bag and then fill each pepper with as much of the cream cheese mixture as will fit. Press the slit edges of the pepper together to seal.

4. Combine the milk, egg, and ½ cup flour in a bowl. Place the panko breadcrumbs and the rest of the flour and Creole seasoning in a separate a shallow bowl and stir to combine.

5. Working in batches, dip the stuffed jalapeños into the milk batter and then roll them in the panko mixture, pressing to coat.

6. Place the stuffed jalapeños on the Crisper Tray. Slide the Crisper Tray into Shelf Position 2. Select the Airfry setting (400° F/205° C). Set the cooking time to 15 mins. Press the Start Button to begin the cooking cycle.

7. Serve with a sprinkle of sea salt.

INGREDIENTS

16 jalapeños

4 oz cream cheese, room temperature

½ cup grated Monterey Jack

6 strips bacon, cooked & crumbled

2 tsp. Creole seasoning (see p. 25)

½ cup milk

1 egg, beaten lightly

½ cup plus 3 tbsp. all-purpose flour

1 ½ cups panko breadcrumbs

sea salt, for serving

Cheese-Stuffed Mushrooms

INGREDIENTS

1 lb large button mushrooms, destemmed

¼ cup extra virgin olive oil, divided

salt, for seasoning

freshly ground black pepper, for seasoning

5.2 oz garlic and herbs Boursin™

3 tbsp. Italian-style breadcrumbs

1 tbsp. finely grated pecorino Romano

1 tbsp. finely chopped parsley

2 tsp. finely chopped fresh basil

DIRECTIONS

1. Use a soft brush to dust any loose dirt off of the mushrooms. Then, brush the mushrooms evenly on all sides with 3 tbsp. olive oil and season lightly on all sides with the salt and black pepper.

2. Use a small spoon or your fingers to fill the cavity in each mushroom cap with some of the Boursin™.

3. Combine the breadcrumbs, pecorino Romano, parsley, and basil with the rest of the olive oil and stir to evenly distribute the oil and herbs. Top each mushroom with some of the breadcrumbs (¼–½ tsp. per mushroom, depending on the size of the mushroom).

4. Place the mushrooms on the Crisper Tray. Slide the Crisper Tray into Shelf Position 5.

5. Select the Airfry setting (400° F/205° C). Set the cooking time to 10 mins. Press the Start Button to begin the cooking cycle.

6. When the mushrooms are done cooking, let them cool for about 3 mins. before carefully transferring them to a serving platter.

Spanakopita

DIRECTIONS

1. Place the spinach in a wire mesh strainer or colander and drain well over a sink. Squeeze the excess water out of the spinach.

2. Place the spinach in a medium-size mixing bowl. Add the salt, black pepper, oregano, parsley, and basil. Stir in the egg, olive oil, and lemon juice. Add the feta and mix well. Reserve the spinach mixture.

3. Gently unfold the filo. Lay 1 filo sheet on a large cutting board and gently brush it with the melted butter. Place a second filo sheet on top of the first and brush with the butter. Repeat two more times until you have a stack of 4 filo sheets with butter brushed between the layers.

4. Use a paring knife to cut each filo sheet lengthwise into three strips. Place 2 tbsp. spinach filling 1 in. from the bottom of each strip. Take the bottom right corner of a strip between your thumb and finger and fold over the spinach filling to the left to make a triangle. Gently pull up the bottom left corner and fold up to make a second triangle. Continue folding until you reach the top. Place the triangle, seam side down, on the Baking Pan. Brush the triangle lightly with butter. Repeat with the rest of the filo until all the filling is used.

5. Place eight triangles on the Crisper Tray and four triangles on the Baking Pan. Slide the Pizza Rack into Shelf Position 1. Place the Baking Pan on top of the Pizza Rack. Slide the Crisper Tray into Shelf Position 2. Select the Bake setting. Set the cooking temperature to 350° F/177° C and set the cooking time to 17 mins. Press the Start Button to begin the cooking cycle.

6. When the cooking time is complete, remove the spanakopita, place the six uncooked triangles on the Crisper Tray in Shelf Position 2, and repeat the cooking process to cook the rest of the spanakopita.

INGREDIENTS

2 10-oz packages frozen chopped spinach, thawed

¼ tsp. salt

⅛ tsp. freshly ground black pepper

1 tsp. dried oregano

1 tsp. dried parsley

1 tsp. dried basil

1 large egg, beaten lightly

2 tbsp. extra virgin olive oil

1 tbsp. fresh lemon juice

1 8-oz package crumbled feta

24 sheets frozen filo pastry, thawed, with a piece of plastic wrap and damp cloth kept over the sheets until ready to use

¾ cups melted unsalted butter

Crab Rangoons

DIRECTIONS

1. Place a small skillet on the stove top. Add the bacon and cook over medium heat until browned and crispy. Then, add the onions, garlic, and ginger and cook while stirring until soft (about 1 min.). Finally, add the crawfish if desired, stir, and remove from the heat.

2. Combine the cooked onion mixture, cream cheese, goat cheese, soy sauce, hot sauce, scallions, and cilantro in a bowl and blend together. Add the Monterey Jack and mix well. Fold in the crabmeat, being careful not to break up the lumps.

3. Place the egg roll wrappers on a work surface. Spoon about ¾ tbsp. of the mixture into the center of one wonton and wet the edges. Fold over the sides to form a triangle and press to seal the edges. Set the wonton on a baking sheet and cover with a lightly damp cloth to prevent the crab rangoons from drying out while filling the rest of the egg roll wrappers.

4. Generously brush the crab rangoons with vegetable oil and evenly divide them between the Crisper Tray and Baking Pan.

5. Slide the Pizza Rack into Shelf Position 1. Place the Baking Pan on top of the Pizza Rack. Slide the Crisper Tray into Shelf Position 2. Select the Bake setting (30-min. cooking time). Set the cooking temperature to 350° F/175° C. Press the Start Button to begin the cooking cycle. Halfway through the cooking time (15 mins.), slide the Baking Pan/Pizza Rack into Shelf Position 2 and slide the Crisper Tray into Shelf Position 5. Cook until the crab rangoons are brown and crispy and warm all the way through.

6. When the cooking time is complete, remove the crab rangoons and serve them with the sweet chile sauce.

INGREDIENTS

4 oz bacon, chopped

¼ cup minced yellow onions

1 tbsp. minced garlic

1 tsp. minced fresh ginger

6 oz crawfish tails (optional)

8 oz cream cheese, softened

4 oz goat cheese, softened

2 tsp. soy sauce

½ tsp. hot pepper sauce

¼ cup chopped scallions

1 tbsp. minced fresh cilantro leaves

2 oz Monterey Jack, grated

1 lb lump crabmeat, picked over for shells & cartilage*

60 wonton wrappers

sweet chile sauce, for serving

* Crawfish can be difficult to find depending on your location. Use 1 ½ lb crabmeat if you do not use the crawfish tails.

Baked Brie

with Pistachios & Apricots

DIRECTIONS

1. Place a medium-size saucepan on the stove top. Combine the apricots, pistachios, honey, water, and thyme in the saucepan and bring the mixture to a brisk simmer over medium heat.

2. Cook while stirring occasionally until the honey becomes thick and syrupy. Then, remove the saucepan from the heat and let cool to room temperature.

3. Roll the pastry sheets using a lightly floured rolling pin into a 16 x 9-in. rectangle and then cut out one 8 ½-in. circle and one 7-in. circle from the pastry.

4. Place the Brie round in the center of the larger pastry circle. Spoon the honey–pistachio mixture over the cheese. Bring the pastry up and around the sides of the cheese, pressing gently to adhere. Brush the top edge of pastry with the egg.

5. Place the 7-in. circle on top of the cheese, pressing around the edge to seal. Brush the top and sides of the pastry with the egg. Cut decorations from the rest of the pastry and arrange them on top. Brush the decorations with the egg.

6. Slide the Pizza Rack into Shelf Position 6. Place the cheese on the Rack. Select the Bake setting (30-min. cooking time). Set the cooking temperature to 350° F/177° C. Press the Start Button to begin the cooking cycle.

7. Transfer the cheese to serving platter and let stand for 20 mins. before serving.

INGREDIENTS

⅓ cup diced dried apricots

⅓ cup chopped toasted pistachios

¼ cup honey

¼ cup water

1 sprig fresh thyme

2 puff pastry sheets, defrosted

1 8-oz Brie round

1 egg, beaten lightly

Pizzas & Calzones

Semolina Pizza Dough

Quick Tomato Sauce

Mini Pizzas with Hot Italian Sausage

Sausage & Roasted Pepper Calzones

Emeril's Margherita Pizza

Emeril's Kicked-Up Calzones al Forno

Wild Mushroom & Manchego Pizza

Calzones with Sopressata & Genoa Salami

New York-Style Thin Crust Pizza

EMERIL LAGASSE

Semolina Pizza Dough

INGREDIENTS

1 ½ cups warm water (about 110° F/43° C)

2 ¼ tsp. active dry yeast

1 tsp. sugar

½ cup olive oil, plus more for greasing

½ cup semolina flour

3 ½ cups unbleached all-purpose flour, plus more for dusting

1 ¼ tsp. salt

DIRECTIONS

1. Combine the warm water, yeast, and sugar in the bowl of a stand mixer fitted with the dough hook. Let the mixture sit until it begins to look creamy or bubbly (about 5 mins.).

2. Add the olive oil, semolina, all-purpose flour, and salt to the yeast mixture and mix on medium speed until the dough is smooth (about 10 mins.), scraping the dough hook midway. Then, transfer the dough to a lightly floured work surface and knead it two to three times with floured hands to form it into a ball.

3. Oil a large mixing bowl, add the dough, turn to coat with oil, and cover the bowl with plastic wrap. Set the bowl aside in a warm, draft-free place until the dough has doubled in size (about 1 hr.).

4. Punch down the dough and allow it to rise a second time until it has doubled in size (about 1 hr.).

5. Divide the dough into either two or four portions (for example, two portions for thick-crust pizza, four portions for calzones or thin-crust pizza), shape the portions into balls, and let them rest for about 15 mins. before either rolling them out to use in a recipe or freezing them for later use.

Quick Tomato Sauce

DIRECTIONS

1. Place a small saucepan on the stove top. Heat the oil over medium heat. Then, add the onion and garlic and cook until soft (about 3 mins.).

2. Add the tomatoes, thyme sprig, salt, and black pepper and simmer for 20 mins. Then, remove the saucepan from the heat.

3. Stir in the extra virgin olive oil, discard the thyme sprig, and reserve the sauce until ready to use.

INGREDIENTS

1 tbsp. olive oil

1 onion, chopped

3 cloves garlic, chopped

1 28-oz can whole peeled tomatoes, drained & puréed

1 sprig fresh thyme

½ tsp. salt

½ tsp. freshly ground black pepper

1 tbsp. extra virgin olive oil

Mini Pizzas
with Hot Italian Sausage

SERVES 4

DIRECTIONS

1. Divide the dough into four equal portions. Lightly dust a work surface with flour. Turn the dough out onto the work surface and roll each dough portion into an 8-in. round.

2. Place the sausage on the Crisper Tray. Slide the Crisper Tray into Shelf Position 2. Select the Airfry setting (400° F/205° C). Set the cooking time to 15 mins. Press the Start Button to begin the cooking cycle.

3. Transfer one dough portion to the Crisper Tray. Spoon one quarter of the tomato sauce evenly over the dough. Sprinkle one quarter of the mozzarella evenly over the sauce. Top the mozzarella with one quarter of the sausage. Garnish with the thyme, crushed red pepper, and Parmigiano-Reggiano.

4. Slide the Crisper Tray into Shelf Position 2. Select the Pizza setting (375° F/191° C) and cook for 15 minutes. If you want a crispier, well done pizza, increase the time by 4–5 minutes. When the first pizza is done cooking, repeat the cooking process with the rest of the pizzas.

5. Serve the pizzas drizzled with the extra virgin olive oil if desired.

INGREDIENTS

1 lb Semolina Pizza Dough (see p. 74)

3 ½ cups Quick Tomato Sauce (see p. 75)

1 ½ lb hot Italian sausage, casings removed & meat crumbled

8 oz mozzarella, grated

2 tbsp. chopped fresh thyme leaves

½ tsp. crushed red pepper

¼ cup finely grated Parmigiano-Reggiano

extra-virgin olive oil, for drizzling (optional)

Sausage & Roasted Pepper Calzones

INGREDIENTS

1 lb Semolina Pizza Dough (see p. 74)

¼ cup thick pesto

1 cup crumbled Italian sausage, cooked

1 red bell pepper, roasted, peeled, seeded & diced

2 tbsp. thinly sliced basil

4 slices fresh mozzarella (½ in. thick)

1 egg, beaten lightly

1 cup marinara or pizza sauce, heated

2 tbsp. grated Parmigiano-Reggiano

DIRECTIONS

1. Divide the dough into four equal portions. Lightly dust a work surface with flour. Turn the dough onto the work surface and roll each portion into an 8-in. round. Spread the pesto over one half of each dough circle.

2. Layer the garlic, sausage, bell pepper, and basil alternately over the pesto. Lay the mozzarella over the basil. Fold the other side of the dough over the filling and pinch the edges to seal the calzones. Make three slashes across the top of each calzone and brush the beaten egg over the calzones.

3. Select the Bake setting. Set the cooking temperature to 400° F/205° C and set the cooking time to 20 mins. Press the Start Button and let the Power AirFryer 360 preheat.

4. When the Power AirFryer 360 has preheated, place two calzones on the Crisper Tray. Slide the Crisper Tray into Shelf Position 2. When the cooking time is complete, repeat the cooking process for the second batch.

5. Serve with the marinara or pizza sauce and the grated Parmigiano-Reggiano.

Emeril's Margherita Pizza

DIRECTIONS

1. Place the dough onto a floured surface. Use a lightly floured rolling pin to roll the dough to fit on the Crisper Tray (about ⅛–¼ in. thick).

2. Spoon the sauce evenly over the dough. Top the sauce with the tomato slices, mozzarella, salt, and black pepper and drizzle with the olive oil.

3. Place the pizza on the Crisper Tray. Slide the Crisper Tray into Shelf Position 5. Select the Pizza setting (375° F/191° C) and cook for 15 minutes. If you want a crispier, well done pizza, increase the time by 4–5 minutes.

4. When the cooking time is complete, slide the Crisper Tray into Shelf Position 1. Select the Pizza setting. Set the cooking temperature to 400° F/205° C and set the cooking time to 2 mins. Press the Start Button to begin the cooking cycle.

5. When the cooking time is complete, top the pizza with the basil. Cut the pizza into six slices and serve immediately.

INGREDIENTS

½ lb Semolina Pizza Dough (see p. 74)

all-purpose flour, for dusting

¼ cup pizza sauce

1 tomato, sliced

4–5 slices fresh mozzarella

salt, to taste

freshly ground black pepper, to taste

olive oil, for drizzling

fresh basil, for serving

Emeril's Kicked-Up Calzones al Forno

DIRECTIONS

1. Combine the tomatoes, olive oil, salt, and black pepper in the bowl of a food processor. Process until smooth and then reserve half of the sauce in a small bowl.

2. Combine the olives, mozzarella cubes, ricotta, Parmesan, sausage, and basil in a small bowl and mix well.

3. Divide the pizza dough into four equal portions. Lightly dust a work surface with flour. Turn the dough out onto the work surface and roll each dough portion into 8-in. rounds.

4. Spread one quarter of the tomato sauce over the bottom half of each dough round, leaving a 1-in. space around the edges. Divide the olive and cheese mixture evenly between the dough rounds. Gently fold the top half of the dough over the filling, rolling and pressing the edges together with your fingertips to seal. Crimp the edges as you go along. Cut a slit in the top of each calzone.

5. Place two calzones on the Crisper Tray. Slide the Crisper Tray into Shelf Position 2. Select the Bake setting. Set the cooking temperature to 400° F/205° C and set the cooking time to 20 mins. Press the Start Button to begin the cooking cycle. When the first batch of calzones are done cooking, repeat the cooking process with the second batch.

6. Serve the calzones with the reserved sauce in the bowl for dipping.

INGREDIENTS

2 cups crushed tomatoes

2 tbsp. olive oil

salt, to taste

black pepper, to taste

⅔ cup Kalamata olives, pitted & coarsely chopped

½ lb mozzarella, cut into ½-in. cubes

½ lb ricotta, drained

¼ cup grated Parmesan

1 cup cooked sausage pieces, such as chorizo or Italian sausage

½ cup chopped fresh basil

1 lb Semolina Pizza Dough (see p. 74)

Wild Mushroom & Manchego Pizza

DIRECTIONS

1. Combine the mushrooms, olive oil, salt, and black pepper in a medium-size bowl and toss. Then, spread the mushrooms in a single layer on the Baking Pan.

2. Slide the Pizza Rack into Shelf Position 1. Place the Baking Pan on top of the Pizza Rack. Select the Airfry setting (400° F/205° C). Set the cooking time to 10 mins. Press the Start Button to begin the cooking cycle. Halfway through the cooking time (5 mins.), stir the mixture.

3. When the cooking time is complete, remove and reserve the mushrooms.

4. Divide the dough into two equal portions. Lightly dust a work surface with flour. Turn the dough out onto the work surface and roll each piece into 8-in. rounds.

5. Place one pizza on the Crisper Tray. Spoon half of the sauce evenly over top the dough. Top the sauce with half of the roasted mushrooms, ham, and Manchego cheese and drizzle the truffle oil over the top of the pizza.

6. Slide the Crisper Tray into Shelf Position 5. Select the Pizza setting (375° F/191° C) and cook for 15 minutes. If you want a crispier, well done pizza, increase the time by 4–5 minutes.

7. When the cooking time is complete, slide the Crisper Tray into Shelf Position 1. Select the Pizza setting. Set the cooking temperature to 400° F/205° C and set the cooking time to 2 mins. Press the Start Button to begin the cooking cycle. When the first pizza is done cooking, repeat the cooking process with the second pizza.

INGREDIENTS

½ lb wild mushrooms, cleaned, destemmed & quartered

1 tbsp. olive oil

salt, to taste

freshly ground pepper, to taste

1 lb Semolina Pizza Dough (see p. 74)

semolina, for dusting, if needed

¼ cup storebought roasted garlic white sauce

4–5 slices Spanish ham, prosciutto, or other thinly sliced cured meat

4–5 slices Manchego cheese

truffle oil, for drizzling

SERVES 4

INGREDIENTS

1 lb Semolina Pizza Dough
(see p. 74)

1 cup Quick Tomato Sauce
(see p. 75)

Filling

1 cup chopped fresh basil
leaves

8 oz mixed sopressata, hot
sopressata, Genoa salami &
pepperoni, chopped

1 cup ricotta, drained

8 oz smoked mozzarella, cut
into ½-in. cubes

¼ cup finely grated
Parmigiano-Reggiano

½ tsp. crushed red pepper

Calzones
with Sopressata & Genoa Salami

DIRECTIONS

1. Divide the pizza dough into four equal portions. Lightly dust a work surface with flour. Turn the dough out onto the work surface and roll each piece into an 8-in. round.

2. Spread ¼ cup tomato sauce over the bottom half of each round, leaving a 1-in. space.

3. Sprinkle ¼ cup of the basil and one quarter of the cured meats evenly over each portion of sauce. Sprinkle one quarter of the ricotta, mozzarella, Parmesan, and crushed red pepper over each portion of meat. Gently fold the top half of the dough over the filling, rolling and pressing the edges together with your fingertips to seal them and crimping as you go along. Cut a slit in the top of each calzone.

4. Place two calzones on the Crisper Tray. Slide the Crisper Tray into Shelf Position 2. Select the Bake setting. Set the cooking temperature to 400° F/205° C and set the cooking time to 20 mins. Press the Start Button to begin the cooking cycle. When the first batch of calzones is done cooking, repeat the cooking process with the second batch.

New York-Style Thin Crust Pizza

DIRECTIONS

1. Divide the dough into two equal portions. Lightly dust a work surface with cornmeal. Turn the dough out onto the work surface and roll each piece into 8-in. rounds.

2. Brush the dough with 2 tbsp. olive oil. Spoon the sauce evenly over the dough, leaving a ½-in. border along the edges. Top the sauce with the basil leaves and then the Parmigiano-Reggiano and mozzarella.

3. Place the Pizza on the Crisper Tray. Slide the Crisper Tray into Shelf Position 5. Select the Pizza setting (375° F/191° C) and cook for 15 minutes. If you want a crispier, well done pizza, increase the time by 4–5 minutes.

4. When the cooking time is complete, slide the Crisper Tray into Shelf Position 1. Select the Pizza setting. Set the cooking temperature to 400° F/205° C and set the cooking time to 2 mins. Press the Start Button to begin the cooking cycle. When the cooking time is complete, repeat the cooking process with the second pizza.

5. When the cooking time is complete, cut the pizza into six slices and serve immediately.

INGREDIENTS

1 lb Semolina Pizza Dough
(see p. 74)

3 ½ cups Quick Tomato Sauce
(see p. 75)

cornmeal, for dusting

¼ cup extra virgin olive oil,
divided

½ cup fresh basil leaves

1 cup freshly grated
Parmigiano-Reggiano

1 lb mozzarella, sliced ¼-inch
thick

Burgers & Sandwiches

Korean Beef Wraps

Turkey Burgers with Cilantro Mayonnaise

French Bread Pizza Sandwiches with Hot
Italian Sausage

Bacon, Mushroom & Onion Burgers

The Veggie–Portobello Burger

Kicked-Up Tuna Melts

Baby Bam Burger

EMERIL LAGASSE

Korean Beef Wraps

DIRECTIONS

1. Combine the soy sauce, orange juice, brown sugar, red pepper flakes, garlic, ginger, white parts of the scallions, and sesame oil in a medium-size bowl and stir together. Then, add the steak and toss to coat.

2. Marinate the steak in the bowl for at least 4 hrs. (up to overnight) in the refrigerator.

3. Once the steak is done marinating, transfer the steak to the Crisper Tray and Baking Pan. Slide the Pizza Rack into Shelf Position 1. Place the Baking Pan on top of the Pizza Rack. Slide the Crisper Tray into Shelf Position 2. Select the Airfry setting (400° F/205° C). Set the cooking time to 10 mins. Press the Start Button to begin the cooking cycle.

4. Serve the steak, rice, kimchi, and miso paste wrapped in the lettuce or with your favorite Korean side dishes if desired.

INGREDIENTS

¼ cup low-sodium soy sauce

2 tbsp. fresh orange juice

1 tbsp. dark brown sugar

1 tbsp. red pepper flakes

1 tbsp. minced garlic

1 tbsp. minced ginger

white parts of 1 bunch scallions, minced

2 tsp. hot sesame oil

1 lb sirloin steak, cut into thin strips about 2 in. long & 1 in. wide

2 tbsp. toasted sesame seeds

steamed white rice, for serving

kimchi, for serving

miso paste, for serving (optional)

Romaine lettuce hearts or butter lettuce, for serving

INGREDIENTS

2 lb ground turkey (preferably a blend of thigh & breast meat)

½ cup minced red onions

¼ cup minced scallions, green parts only

1–2 serrano peppers, minced, to taste

1 egg, whisked

1 tbsp. olive oil

1 tbsp. Worcestershire sauce

1 tbsp. chili powder

1 tsp. hot paprika

1 tsp. ground coriander

1 tsp. ground cumin

Cilantro Mayonnaise

1 large egg yolk

½ tsp. Dijon mustard

¼ cup cilantro leaves

½ tsp. minced garlic

1 cup vegetable oil

2 tbsp. lime juice

½ tsp. salt

¼ tsp. cracked white pepper

---

6 burger buns or potato rolls, warmed in the oven

1 cup grated Monterey Jack

12 small lettuce leaves

12 slices tomato

1 cup thinly sliced red onions

1 avocado, thinly sliced

Turkey Burgers
with Cilantro Mayonnaise

DIRECTIONS

1. Combine the ground turkey, minced onions, peppers, egg, olive oil, Worcestershire sauce, chili powder, paprika, coriander, and cumin in a large bowl and mix.

2. Divide the mixture into six equal portions and use your hands to shape the portions into burgers. Place the burgers on the Crisper Tray. Slide the Crisper Tray into Shelf Position 2.

3. Select the Airfry setting (400° F/205° C for 18 mins.). Press the Start Button to begin the cooking cycle. Cook until the internal temperature of the burgers reaches 165° F/74° C.

4. To make the cilantro mayonnaise, add the egg yolk, mustard, cilantro, and garlic to a food processor. Cover and blend. Slowly drizzle the vegetable oil in a steady stream through the top of the food processor until the mayonnaise reaches a creamy consistency. Then, add the lime juice, salt, and white pepper. Refrigerate the mayonnaise until needed.

5. Serve the burgers on buns with the Monterey Jack, lettuce, tomato, sliced red onions, and avocado. Garnish with the cilantro mayonnaise.

French Bread Pizza Sandwiches

with Hot Italian Sausage

INGREDIENTS

1 ½ lb hot Italian sausage, casings removed & meat crumbled

1 stick unsalted butter

2 tsp. minced garlic

¼ tsp. salt

1 tsp. freshly squeezed lemon juice

1 tbsp. minced fresh parsley leaves

1 loaf French or Italian bread, about 22 in. long

2 cups Quick Tomato Sauce (see p. 75)

8 oz mozzarella, grated

8 oz Fontina, grated

2 tbsp. chopped fresh thyme leaves

½ tsp. crushed red pepper

¼ cup finely grated Parmigiano-Reggiano

extra virgin olive oil, for drizzling (optional)

DIRECTIONS

1. Place a saucepan on the stove top. Heat 1 tbsp. olive oil over medium heat. Add the onion and garlic and cook until soft (about 3 mins.). Add the tomatoes, thyme sprig, salt, and black pepper and simmer for 20 mins. Then, remove the saucepan from the heat, stir in 1 tbsp. extra virgin olive oil, discard the thyme sprig, and reserve the sauce.

2. Place the sausage on the Crisper Tray. Slide the Crisper Tray into Shelf Position 2. Select the Airfry setting (400° F/205° C). Set the cooking time to 10 mins. Press the Start Button to begin the cooking cycle. When the cooking time is complete, remove and reserve the sausage.

3. Place a small pan on the stove top. Melt the butter over medium heat. Then, add the garlic, salt, lemon juice, and parsley to make garlic butter. Remove the garlic butter from the heat.

4. Halve the bread lengthwise and then halve each half crosswise. Scoop out some of the soft part of the thickest portion of the bread, leaving a 1 in.-thick shell. Brush the inside of the bread with the garlic butter.

5. Place the bread, cut side up, on the Pizza Rack. Slide the Pizza Rack into Shelf Position 2. Select the Toast setting (4 mins. 40 secs.) and medium darkness. Press the Start Button to begin the cooking cycle.

6. When the cooking time is complete, remove the toasted bread from the Power AirFryer 360. Spoon the tomato sauce evenly over the pieces of bread. Divide the mozzarella and Fontina evenly over the sauce. Top with the sausage and then garnish with the thyme, crushed red pepper, and Parmigiano-Reggiano.

7. Place the sandwiches on the Pizza Rack. Slide the Pizza Rack into Shelf Position 2. Select the Bake setting (325° F/165° C). Set the cooking time to 10 mins. Press the Start Button to begin the cooking cycle. Cook until the sandwiches are hot and bubbly. Then, drizzle the sandwiches with the extra virgin olive oil if desired and serve.

Bacon, Mushroom & Onion Burgers

DIRECTIONS

1. Place the bacon on the Baking Pan. Slide the Pizza Rack into Shelf Position 1. Place the Baking Pan on top of the Pizza Rack. Select the Airfry setting (400° F/205° C). Set the cooking time to 10 mins. Press the Start Button to begin the cooking cycle.

2. When the cooking time is complete, reserve the bacon on a paper towel-lined plate. Remove and reserve half of the fat from the Baking Pan. Leave the rest of the fat on the Baking Pan.

3. Add the mushrooms to the Baking Pan. Slide the Pizza Rack into Shelf Position 1. Place the Baking Pan on top of the Pizza Rack. Select the Airfry setting (400° F/205° C). Set the cooking time to 6 mins. Press the Start Button to begin the cooking cycle.

4. When the cooking time is complete, reserve the mushrooms on a dish.

5. Add the onions and garlic to the Baking Pan with the reserved bacon fat. Slide the Pizza Rack into Shelf Position 1. Place the Baking Pan on top of the Pizza Rack. Select the Airfry setting (400° F/205° C). Set the cooking time to 10 mins. Press the Start Button to begin the cooking cycle.

6. Combine the mushrooms, onions, and garlic in a small bowl and season with the salt and black pepper.

7. Place the hamburgers on the Crisper Tray. Slide the Crisper Tray into Shelf Position 2. Select the Airfry setting (400° F/205° C). Set the cooking time to 10 mins. Press the Start Button to begin the cooking cycle. Cook until the desired doneness is reached.

8. Place a mound of mushrooms, onions, and Swiss cheese on each hamburger. Select the Airfry setting (400° F/205° C). Set the cooking time to 2 mins. Press the Start Button to begin the cooking cycle.

9. Place the burgers between the toasted buns, top the burgers with the bacon, and dress with the mayonnaise and mustard if desired.

INGREDIENTS

4 slices thick-cut bacon

8 oz shiitake or cremini mushrooms, thinly sliced

1 ½ cups thinly sliced onions

½ tsp. minced garlic

salt, for seasoning

ground black pepper, for seasoning

4 6-oz hamburger patties

4 slices Swiss cheese

4 onion buns, halved & toasted

mayonnaise, for serving (optional)

mustard, for serving (optional)

The Veggie– Portobello Burger

DIRECTIONS

1. Drizzle the olive oil on both sides of the mushroom caps and season them with ½ tsp. salt and ¼ tsp. black pepper.

2. Place the mushroom caps on the Crisper Tray. Slide the Crisper Tray into Shelf Position 2. Select the Airfry setting (400° F/205° C). Set the cooking time to 8 mins. Press the Start Button to begin the cooking cycle.

3. While the mushroom caps cook, place a sauté pan on the stove top. Sweat the onions in the butter over medium heat until caramelized. Then, add the vinegar, honey, thyme, ¼ tsp. salt, and 1 pinch black pepper and reduce until almost dry. Reserve the balsamic onions.

4. Combine the garlic–basil mayonnaise ingredients in a bowl.

5. Spread 2 tsp. garlic–basil mayonnaise on the bottom halves of the buns. Arrange one quarter of the avocado slices on each bottom bun and then add the roasted red peppers and olives. Place the mushroom caps on top of the olives. Spread 2 tbsp. balsamic onions on top of each mushroom. Arrange ¼ cup of the baby spinach on top of the balsamic onions. Place the bun tops on each burger and serve immediately.

INGREDIENTS

¼ cup olive oil

4 portobello mushroom caps, gills removed

½ tsp. salt

¼ tsp. freshly ground black pepper

Balsamic Onions

2 medium onions, sliced

1 tbsp. butter

¼ cup balsamic vinegar

2 tsp. honey

¼ tsp. dried thyme

¼ tsp. salt

1 pinch ground black pepper

Garlic–Basil Mayonnaise

¼ cup mayonnaise

1 tbsp. roasted garlic

1 tbsp. chopped basil

1 tsp. lemon juice

———

4 hamburger buns or kaiser rolls

1 small avocado, peeled, pitted & thinly sliced

½ cup roasted red peppers, thinly sliced

½ cup sliced green queen olives & black ripe olives

1 cup baby spinach

95

Kicked-Up Tuna Melts

INGREDIENTS

2 12-oz cans solid white tuna packed in water, drained

½ cup mayonnaise

⅓ cup chopped red onion

1 ½ tbsp. fresh lemon juice

¼ tsp. dried Italian herbs

½ tsp. fine sea salt

1 tsp. ground black pepper

8 ciabatta bread slices (½ in. thick)

8 thin tomato slices

8 oz provolone cheese, sliced

mixed greens, for serving (optional)

potato chips, for serving (optional)

DIRECTIONS

1. Combine the tuna, mayonnaise, onion, lemon juice, herbs, salt, and black pepper in a bowl.

2. Spoon the tuna evenly on the bread slices and place the bread on the Crisper Tray. Top the tuna with the tomatoes and then the provolone cheese.

3. Slide the Crisper Tray into Shelf Position 2. Select the Airfry setting (400° F/205° C). Set the cooking time to 12 mins. Press the Start Button to begin the cooking cycle.

4. When the cooking time is complete, remove the tuna melts and serve with mixed greens or potato chips.

Baby Bam Burger

MAKES 12

DIRECTIONS

1. Select the Airfry setting (400° F/205° C for 18 mins.). Press the Start Button and let the Power AirFryer 360 preheat.

2. Place the beef in a large mixing bowl. Add the onion, garlic, ketchup, relish, mustard, Creole seasoning, salt, and black pepper and use your hands to mix until all the ingredients are well incorporated.

3. Form the meat into patties, using about 1/4 cup for each. Place the formed patties on the Crisper Tray.

4. When the Power AirFryer 360 has preheated, slide the Crisper Tray into Shelf Position 2.

5. When the cooking time is complete, place the burgers between the buns and top with your favorite accompaniments, such as mayonnaise, mustard, ketchup, onion slices, pickles, pickle relish, tomato slices, and lettuce.

INGREDIENTS

1 ½ lb lean ground beef

½ cup chopped yellow onion

2 tsp. minced garlic

2 tbsp. ketchup

2 tbsp. sweet pickle relish

1 tbsp. yellow mustard

1 tbsp. Creole seasoning (see p. 25)

½ tsp. salt

¼ tsp. ground black pepper

12 small hamburger buns, slider buns, or small dinner rolls

Entrées

Pork & Beef

Poultry

Seafood

EMERIL LAGASSE

Pork & Beef

Filet Mignon with a Blue Cheese Crust

Hanger Steak with a Smoky Paprika Rub

Bone-In Rib Eyes with a Red Wine Sauce

Flank Steak with Chimichurri Sauce

Pork Chops with a Fig Glaze

Pork Medallions with a Dijon Cream Sauce

Caribbean Pork Tenderloins

Stuffed Bacon-Wrapped Pork Tenderloin

Rotisserie Pork Loin with Orange, Cumin & Cilantro

Braised Short Ribs

Filet Mignon
with a Blue Cheese Crust

DIRECTIONS

1. Rub the filets with the olive oil and season them with the salt and black pepper. Place the filets on the Crisper Tray.

2. Slide the Crisper Tray into Shelf Position 2. Select the Airfry setting (400° F/205° C). Set the cooking time to 10 mins. Press the Start Button to begin the cooking cycle. Cook until the desired doneness is reached.

3. When the filets reach the desired doneness, remove them and let them cool. While the steaks are cooling, add the blue cheese, egg yolks, breadcrumbs, cream, lemon juice, and Worcestershire sauce to a bowl and whisk until combined. Top the filets with the blue cheese mixture.

4. Return the filets to the Crisper Tray in Shelf Position 2. Select the Airfry setting (400° F/205° C). Set the cooking time to 5 mins. Press the Start Button to begin the cooking cycle.

5. When the cooking time is complete, remove the filets and let them rest for 5 mins. before serving.

INGREDIENTS

4 6-oz beef filets

1 tbsp. olive oil

1 tsp. kosher salt

½ tsp. freshly ground black pepper

4 oz Gorgonzola or other blue cheese, crumbled

2 egg yolks

¼ cup panko breadcrumbs

1 tbsp. heavy cream

juice of ½ lemon

1 dash Worcestershire sauce

Hanger Steak
with a Smoky Paprika Rub

INGREDIENTS

Smoky Paprika Rub

3 tbsp. pimentón, (preferably pimentón de la Vera, picante)

3 tbsp. salt

1 tbsp. plus 1 tsp. granulated onion powder

2 tsp. granulated garlic powder

2 tsp. ground white pepper

1 ½ tsp. ground black pepper

¼ tsp. dried thyme

¼ tsp. dried oregano

---

2 ¾-lb hanger steaks, membrane trimmed

½ cup vegetable oil

½ cup balsamic vinegar

¼ cup sherry vinegar

½ cup apple juice

1 ½ cups chopped onion

¼ cup chopped garlic

DIRECTIONS

1. Combine the Smoky Paprika Rub ingredients in a small mixing bowl and blend well. The rub can be stored in an airtight container in a cool, dry, dark place for up to 3 months.

2. Place the steaks in a gallon-size plastic resealable food storage bag.

3. Combine the vegetable oil, vinegars, apple juice, onion, garlic, and 2 tbsp. Smoky Paprika Rub in a bowl. Pour the mixture over the steaks in the plastic bag. Transfer the bag to the refrigerator and marinate for at least 6 hrs. (up to overnight). Turn the steaks every few hours.

4. When ready, remove the steaks from the refrigerator and let the steaks come to room temperature (about 1 hr.) Remove the steaks from the bag and season on both sides with more Smoky Paprika Rub.

5. Attach one of the Rotisserie Forks to the Rotisserie Spit and tighten the screws on the Fork. Slide the steaks onto the Spit and into the secured Fork. Secure the steaks on the Spit with the other Fork and screws. Insert the Spit into the Rotisserie connections inside the Power AirFryer 360.

6. Select the Rotisserie setting. Set the cooking temperature to 350° F/175° C and set the cooking time to 20 mins. Press the Start Button to begin the cooking cycle. Cook until the desired doneness is reached (steak is best served rare to medium rare to avoid toughness).

7. When the steaks are done cooking, remove them from the Power AirFryer 360 and let rest for 5 mins. before slicing against the grain for serving.

Bone-In Rib Eyes

with a Red Wine Sauce

DIRECTIONS

1. Season the steaks with the salt and black pepper. Place the steaks on the Pizza Rack. Select the Airfry setting (400° F/205° C for 18 mins.). Press the Start Button and let the Power AirFryer 360 preheat.

2. Once the Power AirFryer 360 has preheated, Slide the Pizza Rack into Shelf Position 2. Cook until the desired doneness is reached (10–12 mins. for medium rare). Then, remove the steaks and let them rest for 10 mins.

3. While the steaks are resting, place a saucepan on the stove top. Melt the butter over medium heat. Add the shallots and garlic, season with the salt and black pepper, and sauté for 1 min.

4. Add the red wine and bring to a boil. Then, reduce the heat to medium, stir in the beef concentrate, and simmer until the beef concentrate has dissolved (about 2 mins.).

5. Add the heavy cream and cook for 1 min. Then, remove the sauce from the heat and keep warm.

6. Slice the steaks and serve with the red wine sauce.

INGREDIENTS

2 1-lb, 1 in.-thick rib eye steaks

salt, to taste, divided

ground black pepper, to taste, divided

1 tbsp. unsalted butter

¼ cup chopped shallots

1 tbsp. minced garlic

½ cup dry red wine

2 tsp. beef concentrate

3 tbsp. heavy cream

Flank Steak

with Chimichurri Sauce

DIRECTIONS

1. Combine the olive oil, sherry vinegar, lime juice, cilantro, basil, marjoram, garlic, and shallots in the bowl of a food processor. Pulse until well blended but not puréed.

2. Add the crushed red pepper, ½ tsp. salt, and ¼ tsp. black pepper and mix to complete the chimichurri sauce.

3. Transfer 1 cup chimichurri sauce from the processor to a nonreactive bowl, cover with plastic wrap, and reserve at room temperature for up to 6 hrs. If cooking the steak another day, refrigerate the sauce and return to room temperature before serving.

4. Season the steak with 1 tsp. salt and ¼ tsp. black pepper on each side and place the steak in a large resealable plastic bag. Add the unreserved chimichurri sauce to the bag. Seal the bag and refrigerate the steak for at least 2 hrs. (up to overnight).

5. When the steak is ready to cook, remove it from the refrigerator and let it sit for 30 mins. to come to room temperature. Brush the excess chimichurri sauce off the steak and then place the steak on the Pizza Rack.

6. Slide the Pizza Rack into Shelf Position 2. Select the Airfry setting (400° F/205° C for 18 mins.). Press the Start Button to begin the cooking cycle. Cook until the desired doneness is reached.

7. Lay the steak on a clean cutting board and let the steak rest for 5–7 mins. before slicing across the grain into thin strips. Serve with crusty bread and the reserved 1 cup chimichurri sauce.

INGREDIENTS

1 cup extra virgin olive oil

⅔ cup sherry wine vinegar

2 tbsp. lime juice

1 cup chopped cilantro

¼ cup chopped fresh basil leaves

1 tbsp. chopped fresh marjoram leaves

3 tbsp. minced garlic

2 tbsp. minced shallots

¼ tsp. crushed red pepper

2 ½ tsp. kosher salt, divided

¾ tsp. fresh cracked black pepper, divided

1 1 ¾–2-lb flank steak

crusty bread, for serving

Pork Chops
with a Fig Glaze

INGREDIENTS

2 12–16-oz thick-cut bone-in pork chops

1 tbsp. olive oil

1 tsp. kosher salt

½ tsp. ground black pepper

1 ½ tbsp. unsalted butter

1 tbsp. minced shallots

1 tsp. minced garlic

⅓ cup fig preserves

¼ cup champagne vinegar

salt, to taste

ground black pepper, to taste

DIRECTIONS

1. Rub the pork chops with the olive oil and season with the kosher salt and black pepper.

2. Place the pork chops on the Pizza Rack. Slide the Pizza Rack into Shelf Position 2. Select the Airfry setting (400° F/205° C). Set the cooking time to 15 mins. Press the Start Button to begin the cooking cycle. Cook until the internal temperature of the pork chops reaches 140° F/60° C (start checking after 12 mins.).

3. While the pork chops are cooking, place a small sauté pan on the stove top. Melt the butter over medium-high heat. Then, add the shallots and garlic and cook until fragrant (about 1 min.).

4. Add the preserves and vinegar and season with the salt and black pepper. Cook until most of the liquid has evaporated and the sauce has a smooth glaze consistency.

5. Serve the pork with the glaze.

Pork Medallions
with a Dijon Cream Sauce

DIRECTIONS

1. Place a small saucepan on the stove top. Melt the butter over medium-low heat.

2. When the butter is bubbling, add the shallots and garlic and cook while stirring until the shallots are soft (about 2 mins.).

3. Add the cream, increase the heat to medium, and cook while stirring occasionally until the cream begins to thicken.

4. Add the mustard, ½ tsp. salt, and ½ tsp. black pepper and cook until the sauce is thick (about 8 mins.).

5. Add the thyme and remove the saucepan from the heat.

6. Season the pork with the rest of the salt and black pepper and drizzle the olive oil over the pork.

7. Place the pork on the Crisper Tray. Slide the Crisper Tray into Shelf Position 2. Select the Airfry setting (400° F/205° C). Set the cooking time to 12 mins. Press the Start Button to begin the cooking cycle. Cook until the medallions are golden brown and cooked through.

8. Transfer the pork to a platter and serve with the cream sauce.

INGREDIENTS

2 tbsp. unsalted butter

1 tbsp. minced shallot

1 tsp. minced garlic

1 cup heavy cream

1 tsp. Dijon mustard

1 tsp. fresh thyme leaves

1 ½ tsp. salt, divided

1 tsp. freshly ground black pepper, divided

1 1 ¼-lb pork tenderloin, cut into 1 ½ in.-thick medallions

1 tbsp. extra virgin olive oil

Caribbean Pork Tenderloins

DIRECTIONS

1. Combine the onion, ginger, garlic, Scotch bonnet chiles, coconut milk, rum, lime juice, and brown sugar in a mixing bowl and whisk to combine to make a marinade.

2. Place the tenderloins inside a gallon-sized resealable plastic food storage bag and add the marinade. Refrigerate for 6 hrs. Turn the tenderloins occasionally while marinating.

3. When ready, remove the tenderloins from the marinade and blot dry with paper towels. Brush the tenderloins with the vegetable oil and season with the salt and black pepper.

4. Attach one of the Rotisserie Forks to the Rotisserie Spit and tighten the screws on the Fork. Slide the tenderloins onto the Spit and into the secured Fork. Secure the tenderloins on the Spit with the other Fork and screws. Tie with twine around the tenderloins in four places. Insert the Spit into the Rotisserie connections inside the Power AirFryer 360.

5. Select the Rotisserie setting. Set the cooking temperature to 350° F/175° C and set the cooking time to 40 mins. Press the Start Button to begin the cooking cycle.

6. When the tenderloins are done cooking, remove and let rest for 10 mins. before slicing and serving. Garnish with the cilantro.

INGREDIENTS

½ small Vidalia onion, sliced

¼ cup minced ginger

2 tbsp. minced garlic

2 Scotch bonnet chiles, ribbed, seeded, destemmed & minced

1 14-oz can unsweetened coconut milk

½ cup dark rum

¼ cup lime juice

3 tbsp. cane or dark brown sugar

2 1-lb pork tenderloins, trimmed of fat

vegetable oil, for brushing

1 tsp. kosher salt

½ tsp. freshly ground black pepper

1 tbsp. freshly chopped cilantro

Stuffed Bacon-Wrapped

Pork Tenderloin

DIRECTIONS

1. Pound the tenderloin with a meat mallet until each is ½ in. thick. Reserve the tenderloin in the refrigerator.

2. Place a medium-size skillet on the stove top. Dice 2 bacon slices and cook them over medium heat until browned (about 15 mins.). Add the onions and celery and sauté until the onions are translucent (about 5 mins.). Add the garlic and sauté for 2 mins. Add the stock, cranberries, thyme, 1 tsp. salt, and ¾ tsp. black pepper, bring the mixture to a simmer, and remove the skillet from the heat. Stir in the stuffing until moist and the ingredients are evenly distributed. Let cool.

3. Combine the honey, soy sauce, and chipotle in a small bowl and stir until the mixture is combined to make a glaze. Reserve the glaze.

4. Spread the stuffing lengthwise across three quarters of the tenderloin, leaving about 1 in. bare at one end. Starting with the stuffing-filled ends, roll the tenderloin firmly lengthwise (be careful not to squeeze out the stuffing). Secure the tenderloin closed with toothpicks.

5. Wrap 3 bacon slices around the tenderloin. Tie the tenderloin with twine, leaving 1 in. between each loop, to secure the bacon and stuffing. Remove the toothpicks and season with the salt and black pepper.

6. Attach one of the Rotisserie Forks to the Rotisserie Spit and tighten the screws on the Fork. Slide the tenderloin onto the Spit and into the secured Fork and tie the tenderloin with twine (about 4 loops 2 in. apart). Secure the tenderloin on the Spit with the other Fork and screws. Insert the Spit into the Rotisserie connections inside the Power AirFryer 360. Select the Rotisserie setting. Set the cooking temperature to 340° F/171° C and set the cooking time to 40 mins. Press the Start Button to begin the cooking cycle.

7. When the cooking time is complete, brush the tenderloin with the glaze and let rest for 5–10 mins. before carving.

INGREDIENTS

1 1–1 ¼ lb pork tenderloin, butterflied in half lengthwise

4 bacon slices, divided

¼ cup finely diced onions

⅛ cup finely diced celery

1 clove garlic, minced

½ cup chicken stock

¼ cup dried cranberries

½ tsp. chopped fresh thyme

1 tsp. salt, divided

1 tsp. ground black pepper, divided

2 cups soft, cubed unflavored stuffing

¼ cup honey

2 tsp. soy sauce

1 tsp. canned chipotle peppers in adobo, minced

Rotisserie Pork Loin

with Orange, Cumin & Cilantro

INGREDIENTS

1 3 ½-lb pork loin

2 tbsp. olive oil

1 tbsp. kosher salt

1½ tsp. ground cumin

1½ tsp. ground black pepper

½ cup freshly squeezed orange juice

¼ cup freshly squeezed lime juice

¼ cup white wine vinegar

2 tbsp. orange marmalade

2 tbsp. chopped fresh cilantro

DIRECTIONS

1. Rub the pork loin well on all sides with the olive oil and season with the salt, cumin, and black pepper.

2. Attach one of the Rotisserie Forks to the Rotisserie Spit and tighten the screws on the Fork. Slide the pork loin onto the Spit and into the secured Fork. Secure the pork loin on the Spit with the other Fork and screws. Insert the Spit into the Rotisserie connections inside the Power AirFryer 360.

3. Select the Rotisserie setting. Set the cooking temperature to 340° F/171° C and set the cooking time to 1 hr. Press the Start Button to begin the cooking cycle.

4. Combine the orange juice, lime juice, white wine vinegar, orange marmalade, and cilantro in a medium-size bowl and whisk well to combine. Baste the pork with the mixture every 10 mins. while it is cooking.

5. When the pork is done cooking, let it rest for 7–10 mins. before slicing thinly.

6. Drizzle the pork with the pan drippings from the Drip Tray.

Braised
Short Ribs

DIRECTIONS

1. Place a 4 ½-qt. Dutch oven that fits in the Power AirFryer 360 on the stove top. Heat the vegetable oil over high heat. While the oil heats up, season the ribs with the Creole seasoning, patting the seasoning in well with your hands. When the oil is nearly smoking, add the ribs without crowding them (in batches if necessary) and sear on all sides until they form a brown crust. When all the ribs have browned, transfer them to the Baking Pan.

2. Reduce the heat and add the onions, celery, carrots, and garlic to the Dutch oven and cook for 4–5 mins. to brown lightly. Then, return the ribs to the Dutch oven and add the tomatoes, vinegar, Worcestershire sauce, bay leaves, pepper and enough broth to just cover the ribs and stir. Bring the mixture to a boil and then reduce the heat to gently simmering.

3. Cover the Dutch oven. Slide the Pizza Rack into Shelf Position 6. Place the Dutch oven on the Pizza Rack. Select the Slow Cook setting (225° F/107° C). Set the cooking time to 6 hrs. Press the Start Button to begin the cooking cycle.

4. When the cooking time is complete, place the ribs in the center of four plates, spoon the sauce over the ribs, and garnish with chopped scallion greens.

INGREDIENTS

2 tbsp. vegetable oil

3 ½ lb short ribs

2 tbsp. Creole seasoning

1 cup chopped onions

½ cup chopped celery

½ cup chopped carrots

2 tbsp. chopped garlic

1 cup peeled, seeded & chopped tomatoes

½ cup red wine vinegar

2 tbsp. Worcestershire sauce

3 bay leaves

1 tsp. ground black pepper

1 qt. beef broth

¼ cup chopped scallion greens, for sprinkling

Poultry

Pecan-Crusted Chicken Fingers
with Honey Mustard Dipping Sauce

Chicken Tenders with Zesty Dipping Sauce

Adobo Chicken Thighs

Braised Chicken Thighs with Lemon
& Rosemary

Emeril's "Jerk" Chicken with Gingered
BBQ Drizzle

Roast Chicken with Shallot–Garlic Butter

Cornish Game Hens with Honey,
Lemon & Thyme

Creole-Seasoned Cornish Hens

Split Chicken Breasts Marinated in Garlic
& Oregano

Bacon & Herbs Turkey Breast

Roasted Chicken with Lemon Herb Sauce

Oven-Roasted Chicken with Garlic–
Rosemary Smear

Turkey Roulade with Peach & Sage Gravy

Crispy Rotisserie Chicken
with Garlic–Thyme Butter

EMERIL LAGASSE

Pecan-Crusted Chicken Fingers

with Honey Mustard Dipping Sauce

DIRECTIONS

1. Combine the pecans, breadcrumbs, and 2 tsp. Creole seasoning in the bowl of a food processor and pulse for 1 min. to combine. Pour the mixture into a shallow dish.

2. Beat together the eggs, olive oil, and the rest of the Creole seasoning in a bowl. One at a time, dip the chicken into the egg mixture and then dredge them in the pecan mixture, shaking to remove any excess.

3. Place the chicken on the Baking Pan and Crisper Tray. Slide the Pizza Rack into Shelf Position 1. Place the Baking Pan on top of the Pizza Rack. Slide the Crisper Tray into Shelf Position 2. Select the Airfry setting. Set the cooking temperature to 360° F/182° C and set the cooking time to 15 mins. Press the Start Button to begin the cooking cycle. Halfway through the cooking time (7 ½ mins.), slide the Crisper Tray into Shelf Position 5 and slide the Baking Pan/Pizza Rack into Shelf Position 2.

4. While the chicken cooks, combine the honey mustard dipping sauce ingredients in a bowl and whisk to combine.

5. When the chicken is done cooking, season it lightly with the salt and serve with the dipping sauce.

INGREDIENTS

1 cup pecan pieces

½ cup breadcrumbs

1 tbsp. plus 1 tsp. Creole seasoning (see p. 25)

2 large eggs

¼ cup olive oil

2 lb boneless & skinless chicken breasts, cut lengthwise into strips

Honey Mustard Dipping Sauce

½ cup mayonnaise

2 tbsp. honey

2 tbsp. Creole mustard or other hot whole-grain mustard

1 pinch salt

1 pinch ground cayenne pepper

---

salt, to taste

Chicken Tenders

with Zesty Dipping Sauce

INGREDIENTS

¾ lb chicken tenders

½ tsp. salt

¼ tsp. ground black pepper

½ cup flour

1 tbsp. Creole seasoning (see p. 25)

2 tbsp. milk

1 large egg

1 cup panko breadcrumbs

2 tbsp. vegetable oil

Zesty Dipping Sauce

½ cup mayonnaise

2 tbsp. ketchup

2 tbsp. Louisiana hot sauce

1 tsp. Dijon mustard

1 tsp. Worcestershire sauce

½ tsp. garlic powder

¼ tsp. ground black pepper

¼ tsp. ground cayenne pepper

DIRECTIONS

1. Season the chicken with the salt and black pepper and reserve the chicken.

2. Combine the flour and 1 tsp. Creole seasoning in a small bowl. Combine the milk, egg, and 1 tsp. Creole seasoning in a second small bowl. Combine the panko breadcrumbs and 1 tsp. Creole seasoning in a third small bowl.

3. Dredge the chicken in the flour, turning to coat evenly. Then, dip the chicken in the milk mixture, turning to coat evenly. Remove the chicken from the milk mixture, allowing the excess milk to drip off, and then dredge the chicken in the breadcrumbs. Set the chicken on the Crisper Tray, drizzle the vegetable oil over the chicken, and turn to coat evenly.

4. Slide the Crisper Tray into Shelf Position 2. Select the Airfry setting. Set the cooking temperature to 360° F/182° C and set the cooking time to 15 mins. Press the Start Button to begin the cooking cycle.

5. While the chicken is cooking, combine the Zesty Dipping Sauce ingredients in a bowl and mix.

6. When the cooking time is complete, remove the chicken and serve immediately with the sauce.

Adobo Chicken Thighs

DIRECTIONS

1. Place the chicken thighs in a resealable plastic food storage bag along with the garlic, bay leaves, 3 tbsp. vinegar, and 3 tbsp. soy sauce. Seal the bag and move the thighs around to distribute the marinade evenly. Refrigerate the chicken in the bag for at least 4 hrs. (up to overnight).

2. When the chicken is done marinating, let it return to room temperature (about 1 hr.). Then, remove the chicken from the marinade, brush the thighs on both sides with the olive oil, and season both sides with the salt and black pepper.

3. Place the chicken on the Crisper Tray. Slide the Crisper Tray into Shelf Position 5. Select the Airfry setting. Set the cooking temperature to 350° F/177° C and set the cooking time to 25 mins. Press the Start Button to begin the cooking cycle. Cook until the chicken is golden brown and cooked through.

4. While the chicken is cooking, place a very small saucepan on the stove top. Combine the honey and the rest of the vinegar and soy sauce and bring to a simmer over medium heat. Cook until the mixture becomes thickened to a consistency that coats the back of a spoon, taking care not to over-reduce the liquid, which will easily burn. Then, remove the mixture from the heat.

5. Let chicken rest for at least 5 mins. before serving. Serve the chicken drizzled with the reduced vinegar–soy mixture.

INGREDIENTS

8 6–7-oz bone-in chicken thighs

3 tbsp. minced garlic

4 bay leaves

1 cup plus 3 tbsp. cider vinegar, divided

½ cup plus 2 tbsp. soy sauce, divided

2 tbsp. olive oil

salt, to taste

freshly ground black pepper, to taste

4 tbsp. honey

Braised Chicken Thighs
with Lemon & Rosemary

DIRECTIONS

1. Brush the chicken thighs on both sides with the olive oil and then sprinkle both sides of the chicken with the salt, black pepper, and 2 tbsp. flour.

2. Scatter the sliced shallots, lemon slices, garlic, and rosemary along the bottom of the Baking Pan and top with the chicken thighs, skin side up.

3. Slide the Pizza Rack into Shelf Position 1. Place the Baking Pan on top of the Pizza Rack. Select the Airfry setting (400° F/205° C). Set the cooking time to 12 mins. Press the Start Button to begin the cooking cycle. Cook until the chicken is lightly golden and crispy around the top edges.

4. Transfer the chicken to a casserole dish along with the shallots, lemon, garlic, and rosemary. Sprinkle the olives over the top of the chicken.

5. Combine the broth, wine, cream, anchovies, and crushed red pepper in a bowl and whisk together. Pour the mixture over the chicken.

6. Slide the Pizza Rack into Shelf Position 5. Place the casserole dish on the Pizza Rack. Select the Bake setting. Set the cooking temperature to 350° F/175° C and set the cooking time to 25 mins. Press the Start Button to begin the cooking cycle. Every 10 mins., rearrange the chicken so that the pieces are evenly browned on top.

7. When the cooking time is complete, transfer the chicken to a serving dish and leave the cooking liquid in the casserole dish.

8. Blend the butter with the rest of the flour to form a smooth paste in a small heatproof bowl. Ladle about ½ cup of the hot cooking liquid into the bowl and whisk to blend.

9. Stir the paste mixture into the rest of the cooking liquid in the casserole dish. The juices should thicken immediately. Taste and adjust the seasoning with the salt and black pepper if necessary. Then, pour the sauce over the chicken and serve immediately.

INGREDIENTS

4 boneless chicken thighs, extra skin & fat trimmed

1 tsp. extra virgin olive oil

kosher salt, to taste, divided

freshly ground black pepper, to taste, divided

3 tbsp. instant flour, divided

2 large shallots, sliced

4 lemon slices

4 garlic cloves, crushed

2–3 fresh rosemary sprigs

½ cup pitted Kalamata olives

1 ¼ cups chicken broth

½ cup dry white wine

2 tbsp. heavy cream

¾ tsp. finely chopped anchovies

¼ tsp. crushed red pepper

1 tbsp. unsalted butter, at room temperature

cooked pasta, rice, or crusty French bread, for serving

INGREDIENTS

12–14 scallions (white parts only), chopped (about ¾ cup)

8 Scotch bonnet or habanero chiles, stems & seeds removed

⅓ cup minced garlic

⅓ cup minced ginger

¼ cup freshly squeezed lime juice

3 tbsp. dark rum

3 tbsp. soy sauce

2 tbsp. light brown sugar

1 tbsp. fresh thyme leaves

2 tbsp. pumpkin pie spice

2 boneless chicken thighs

2 boneless chicken breasts, cut in half

vegetable oil, for brushing

½ tbsp. kosher salt

Gingered BBQ Drizzle

¼ cup plus 2 tbsp. ketchup

1 tbsp. Worcestershire sauce

¼ cup pineapple juice

1 tbsp. butter

2 tbsp. fresh lime juice

2 tbsp. vinegar

¼ cup firmly packed brown sugar

2 tbsp. minced fresh ginger

1 tbsp. tamarind pulp

1 tsp. salt

1 tsp. dry mustard

1 tsp. minced garlic

½ Scotch bonnet chiles, seeded & minced

Emeril's "Jerk" Chicken
with Gingered BBQ Drizzle

DIRECTIONS

1. Combine the scallions, chiles, garlic, ginger, lime juice, rum, soy sauce, brown sugar, thyme, and pumpkin pie spice in a food processor and process to form a smooth paste.

2. Place the chicken in a gallon-sized resealable plastic food storage bag. Add the marinade and seal. Refrigerate for at least 4 hrs. (up to 24 hrs.). Turn the chicken occasionally.

3. When ready, remove the chicken from the marinade and discard the marinade. Wipe the chicken with clean paper towels to remove any excess marinade and then brush with the vegetable oil. Season the chicken on both sides with the salt.

4. Attach one of the Rotisserie Forks to the Rotisserie Spit and tighten the screws on the Fork. Slide the chicken onto the Spit and into the secured Fork. Secure the chicken on the Spit with the other Fork and screws. Insert the Spit into the Rotisserie connections inside the Power AirFryer 360.

5. Select the Rotisserie setting (30-min. cooking time). Set the cooking temperature to 340° F/171° C. Press the Start Button to begin the cooking cycle.

6. While the chicken cooks, place a small saucepan on the stove top. Combine the Gingered BBQ Drizzle ingredients and cook over medium heat until reduced enough to coat the back of a spoon (about 10 mins.).

7. When the chicken is done, remove it from the Power AirFryer 360 and let it rest for 5 mins. before serving with the Gingered BBQ Drizzle.

Roast Chicken

with Shallot–Garlic Butter

DIRECTIONS

1. Combine the butter, shallots, parsley, garlic, ¼ tsp. salt, and ¼ tsp. black pepper.

2. Rub 1 tbsp. flavored butter on the inside of the chicken and sprinkle the cavity with ¼ tsp. salt and ¼ tsp. black pepper.

3. Use your fingers to gently loosen the skin covering the breast and place ½ tbsp. flavored butter under the skin on each side of the breast (working from the top end) and under the skin of each thigh (working from the bottom end of the breast). Reserve any extra flavored butter for brushing on the chicken when finished if desired.

4. Tuck the wings behind the bird and tie the leg ends together with kitchen twine. Sprinkle the rest of the salt and black pepper all over the chicken.

5. Attach one of the Rotisserie Forks to the Rotisserie Spit and tighten the screws on the Fork. Slide the chicken onto the Spit and into the secured Fork and tie with twine around the breast and then around the legs. Secure the chicken on the Spit with the other Fork and screws. Insert the Spit into the Rotisserie connections inside the Power AirFryer 360.

6. Select the Rotisserie setting. Set the cooking temperature to 340° F/171° C and set the cooking time to 35 mins. Press the Start Button to begin the cooking cycle. Cook until the internal temperature of the chicken reaches 165° F/74° C.

7. When the chicken is done cooking, transfer it to a cutting board and let rest for 10 mins.

8. Brush the warm chicken with the rest of the flavored butter. Then, carve and serve with the pan juices spooned over the top.

INGREDIENTS

3 tbsp. unsalted butter, at room temperature

2 tbsp. minced shallots

1 tbsp. chopped fresh parsley

1 tsp. minced garlic

1 ½ tsp. salt, divided

¾ tsp. freshly ground black pepper, divided

1 3 ½-lb chicken, rinsed & patted dry, excess fat & giblets removed

Cornish Game Hens

with Honey, Lemon & Thyme

DIRECTIONS

1. Rinse the inside and outside of the hens well under cool running water. Pat them dry with paper towels.

2. Combine the thyme, lemon zest, and ¼ cup butter in a small bowl and use a fork to blend well. Divide the mixture into four portions and spread one portion under the skin of each hen, covering the breast. Combine 1 tsp. salt with ½ tsp. black pepper and season the cavities of the hens. Truss the hens and fold the wing tips back.

3. Attach one of the Rotisserie Forks to the Rotisserie Spit and tighten the screws on the Fork. Slide two of the hens onto the Spit and into the secured Fork. Secure the hens on the Spit with the other Fork and screws. Insert the Spit into the Rotisserie connections inside the Power AirFryer 360.

4. Select the Rotisserie setting (30-min. cooking time). Set the cooking temperature to 340° F/171° C. Press the Start Button to begin the cooking cycle. Cook until the internal temperature of the hens reaches 165° F/74° C.

5. While the hens cook, place a small saucepan on the stove top. Combine the lemon juice, honey, soy sauce, and the rest of the butter in the saucepan and warm over low heat until heated through. Reserve half of the honey mixture and use some of the rest to baste the tops of the hens well. Season the hens with the rest of the salt and black pepper.

6. When the hens are done cooking, remove them from the Power AirFryer 360 and let them rest for about 5 mins. Repeat the cooking process with the other two hens. Discard the honey mixture used for basting and drizzle the reserved honey mixture over the hens before serving.

INGREDIENTS

4 Cornish game hens

1 tbsp. plus 1 tsp. chopped fresh thyme

grated zest of 2 lemons

1 stick butter, divided

1 tbsp. plus 1 tsp. salt, divided

1 tsp. freshly ground black pepper, divided

2 tbsp. freshly squeezed lemon juice

⅓ cup honey

1 tbsp. plus 1 tsp. soy sauce

Creole-Seasoned Cornish Hens

INGREDIENTS

2 1 ½-lb Cornish game hens

2 tbsp. olive oil

2 ½ tsp. Creole seasoning (see p. 25)

1 tsp. kosher salt

1 lemon, halved

10 sprigs fresh thyme

DIRECTIONS

1. Rub the Cornish hens with the olive oil and season them with the Creole seasoning and salt. Place a lemon half and 5 thyme sprigs in each cavity of each hen. Tie the hen so that the wings are pinned behind the back and the legs are pushed together and up.

2. Attach one of the Rotisserie Forks to the Rotisserie Spit and tighten the screws on the Fork. Slide the hens onto the Spit and into the secured Fork. Secure the hens on the Spit with the other Fork and screws. Insert the Spit into the Rotisserie connections inside the Power AirFryer 360.

3. Select the Rotisserie setting (30-min. cooking time). Set the cooking temperature to 340° F/171° C. Press the Start Button to begin the cooking cycle. Cook until the internal temperature of the hens reaches 165° F/74° C.

4. Let the hens rest for 5 mins. before carving.

Split Chicken Breasts

Marinated in Garlic & Oregano

DIRECTIONS

1. Combine the olive oil, oregano, garlic, lemon zest, salt, and ground cayenne pepper in a small bowl. Spread a little of the mixture under the skin of the chicken and the rest over the skin. Place the chicken in a resealable plastic bag and marinate the chicken in the refrigerator overnight.

2. When the chicken is done marinating, place it on the Crisper Tray. Slide the Crisper Tray into Shelf Position 2. Select the Bake setting (325° F/165° C for 30 mins.). Press the Start Button to begin the cooking cycle. Cook until the internal temperature of the chicken reaches 165° F/74° C.

3. Let the chicken rest for 5 mins. before removing the breast from the bone and slicing.

INGREDIENTS

¼ cup extra virgin olive oil

1 tbsp. dried oregano

4 cloves garlic, sliced

½ tsp. lemon zest

¾ tsp. kosher salt

¼ tsp. ground cayenne pepper

2 lb split chicken breast halves, about ¾ lb each

Bacon & Herb Turkey Breast

DIRECTIONS

1. Place a medium-size skillet on the stove top. Cook the bacon until crisp over medium-high heat. Reserve 1 tbsp. bacon fat and transfer the bacon to paper towels to drain.

2. When the bacon has cooled, chop it finely and transfer it to a small bowl. Add the garlic, sage, rosemary, oregano, thyme, butter, 1 tsp. salt, and ½ tsp. black pepper. Use a small spoon to mix thoroughly to combine and form a paste.

3. Use your fingertips to gently loosen the skin on the turkey breast so that the skin is separated from the flesh. Gently spread the herb paste between the skin and flesh. Season the outside of the turkey breast with the rest of the salt and black pepper. Brush the turkey all over with the reserved bacon fat.

4. Place the turkey on the Crisper Tray. Slide the Crisper Tray into Shelf Position 2. Select the Bake setting (325° F/165° C for 30 mins.). Press the Start Button to begin the cooking cycle. Cook until the internal temperature of the hens reaches 165° F/74° C.

5. When the cooking time is complete, remove the turkey from the Power AirFryer 360 and let rest for 20 mins. before carving into thin slices.

6. Serve with the pan drippings from the Drip Tray.

INGREDIENTS

3 strips thick-cut bacon

1 ½ tbsp. minced garlic

1 tbsp. chopped fresh sage

1 ½ tsp. chopped fresh rosemary

1 tsp. chopped fresh oregano

1 tsp. chopped fresh thyme

3 tbsp. unsalted butter, softened

2 tsp. kosher salt, divided

1 tsp. freshly ground black pepper, divided

1 2 ½–3-lb half turkey breast, rinsed & patted dry

Roasted Chicken

with Lemon Herb Sauce

INGREDIENTS

1 3–3 ½-lb chicken, rinsed well, patted dry & giblets removed

salt, to taste

freshly ground black pepper, to taste

½ cup plus 2 tbsp. olive oil, divided

8 sprigs fresh thyme

1 cup chicken stock

2 tsp. Dijon mustard

2 tbsp. fresh lemon juice

1 tbsp. assorted chopped fresh herbs, such as basil, parsley, chives & oregano

fresh parsley leaves, for garnish

DIRECTIONS

1. Season the chicken generously inside and out with the salt and black pepper and rub the chicken with 2 tbsp. olive oil. Place the thyme in the cavity of the chicken and use butcher's twine to tie the legs together. Tie a piece of twine around the breast and again around the legs.

2. Attach one of the Rotisserie Forks to the Rotisserie Spit and tighten the screws on the Fork. Slide the chicken onto the Spit and into the secured Fork. Secure the chicken on the Spit with the other Fork and screws. Insert the Spit into the Rotisserie connections inside the Power AirFryer 360.

3. Select the Rotisserie setting. Set the cooking temperature to 340° F/171° C and set the cooking time to 35 mins. Press the Start Button to begin the cooking cycle. Cook until the internal temperature of the chicken reaches 165° F/74° C.

4. While the chicken cooks, place a small saucepan on the stove top. Combine the stock and Dijon mustard and bring to a brisk simmer over medium heat. Then, remove the saucepan from the heat.

5. Whisk in the lemon juice, herbs, and the rest of the olive oil. Transfer the lemon herb sauce to a gravy boat or measuring cup and cover to keep warm until ready to serve. Garnish with the parsley.

Oven-Roasted Chicken

with Garlic–Rosemary Smear

DIRECTIONS

1. Place the roasted garlic, chopped rosemary, and 1 ½ tbsp. olive oil in a food processor and purée until very smooth. Season with the salt and white pepper.

2. Place the potatoes and onions on the Baking Pan and drizzle 3 tbsp. olive oil over the potatoes and onions. Toss to ensure the vegetables are nicely coated in oil and then season with the salt and white pepper. Add all but one of the rosemary sprigs to the pan.

3. Place a large nonstick skillet on the stove top. Heat the skillet over medium-high heat. Then, brown the chicken on all sides.

4. Season the chicken generously with the salt and white pepper. Carefully transfer the chicken to the Baking Pan, positioning the chicken over the potatoes and onions. Spoon 2 tbsp. garlic–rosemary purée over the chicken and use the back of a spoon to spread the purée evenly all over the chicken.

5. Slide the Pizza Rack into Shelf Position 1. Place the Baking Pan on top of the Pizza Rack. Select the Roast setting (350° F/175° C for 1 hr.). Press the Start Button to begin the cooking cycle. Cook until the internal temperature of the chicken reaches 165° F/74° C. Then, remove the chicken and let rest for 10 mins.

6. Place a sauté pan on the stove top. Heat the pan over medium-high heat, add the wine, and cook until nearly completely reduced. Add the stock and the juices from the chicken and cook until reduced by half. Whisk in 2 tbsp. garlic–rosemary purée, simmer, and whisk in the cold butter cubes little by little. Do not let boil or the sauce will separate.

7. Place the potatoes in a dish. Slice the chicken, transfer the chicken to the dish with the potatoes, and drizzle the sauce over the chicken. Any leftover garlic–rosemary purée can be used to flavor mashed potatoes, soup, or gravy.

INGREDIENTS

4 heads of roasted garlic

1 tbsp. chopped rosemary, plus several whole sprigs, divided

¼ cup plus 2 tbsp. olive oil, divided

salt, to taste

white pepper, to taste

1 4-lb chicken

1 ½ lb new potatoes, quartered or halved if large

2 onions, peeled & quartered

¾ cup dry white wine

1 ½ cups chicken stock

¼ cup cold unsalted butter, cubed

Turkey Roulade

with Peach & Sage Gravy

DIRECTIONS

1. Combine the water, sugar, and ¾ cup kosher salt in a stock pot and whisk until the sugar and salt dissolve. Refrigerate the turkey in the pot for 8 hrs.

2. Drain the turkey breast and pat dry. Lay three 32-in. strings of twine lengthwise across a cutting board. Pull the turkey skin down to cover as much of the breast meat as possible. Lay the turkey breast (skin side down) on the strings. Cover the turkey with parchment paper and pound until the thickest part of the breast is no more than 2 in. thick.

3. Combine the breadcrumbs, bacon, bacon fat, butter, garlic, parsley, and Creole seasoning in a bowl to make stuffing. Lightly season the turkey breast with the Creole seasoning. Stuff the turkey breast with 3 tightly packed cups of the stuffing. Roll the breast in one direction to form a tight cylinder. Tie the breast together in three places. Brush with ¼ cup olive oil and season with the Creole seasoning, salt, and black pepper.

4. Attach one of the Rotisserie Forks to the Rotisserie Spit and tighten the screws on the Fork. Slide the turkey onto the Spit and into the secured Fork. Secure the turkey on the Spit with the other Fork and screws. Insert the Spit into the Rotisserie connections inside the Power AirFryer 360. Select the Rotisserie setting. Set the cooking temperature to 350° F/175° C and set the cooking time to 45 mins. Press the Start Button to begin the cooking cycle. Cook until the internal temperature of the turkey reaches 160° F/71° C.

5. While the turkey cooks, place a 2-qt. saucepan on the stove top. Heat 2 tbsp. olive oil over medium heat. Add the shallots and garlic and sauté while stirring often until the shallots are fragrant and lightly caramelized (about 1 min.).Add the white wine vinegar to the pan and cook until it is nearly completely reduced (about 1 min.). Then, add the stock and preserves to the saucepan and raise the heat to high.

6. While the sauce comes to a boil, combine the butter and flour in a bowl and blend to form a smooth paste. Add the paste to the sauce and use a whisk to stir the paste in, ensuring that it is well distributed.

7. Bring the sauce to a boil and season with 1 ¼ tsp. salt and ¾ tsp. black pepper. Then, reduce to a simmer and reduce by one quarter (about 20 mins.). Add the sage and let steep for about 3 mins. before straining.

8. Remove the cooked turkey and let rest for 10 mins. Slice crosswise into ½-in. slices. Serve with the Peach and Sage Gravy.

INGREDIENTS

1 gallon water

1 cup brown sugar

¾ cup kosher salt, plus more for seasoning

1 3-lb boneless turkey breast, skin on

1 loaf of French or Italian bread, coarsely chopped in a food processor (4 cups breadcrumbs)

½ lb bacon, chopped & cooked in a pan until crisp, fat reserved

¼ cup reserved bacon fat

2 tbsp. unsalted butter, melted

2 tbsp. chopped garlic

½ cup chopped parsley

1 tsp. Creole seasoning, plus more for seasoning (see p. 25)

¼ cup olive oil

ground black pepper, for seasoning

Peach & Sage Gravy

2 tbsp. olive oil

¼ cup finely minced shallots

2 tsp. minced garlic

½ cup white wine vinegar

4 cups turkey stock, chicken stock, or canned low-sodium chicken broth

¾ cup peach preserves

2 tbsp. unsalted butter

2 tbsp. all-purpose flour

1 ¼ tsp. salt

¾ tsp. ground black pepper

⅓ cup sage leaves

Crispy Rotisserie Chicken

with Garlic–Thyme Butter

DIRECTIONS

1. Season the chicken halves on both sides with the salt and white pepper.

2. Attach one of the Rotisserie Forks to the Rotisserie Spit and tighten the screws on the Fork. Slide the chicken onto the Spit and into the secured Fork with tie the chicken with twine. Secure the chicken on the Spit with the other Fork and screws. Insert the Spit into the Rotisserie connections inside the Power AirFryer 360.

3. Select the Rotisserie setting. Set the cooking temperature to 340° F/171° C and set the cooking time to 40 mins. Press the Start Button to begin the cooking cycle.

4. While the chicken is roasting, combine the butter, garlic, and thyme in a small bowl and stir well to blend.

5. As soon as the chicken is removed from the Power AirFryer 360, spread the garlic butter over the skin and serve immediately.

INGREDIENTS

1 3 ½-lb chicken

1 tbsp. kosher salt

1 ½ tsp. freshly ground white pepper

1 tbsp. plus 1 tsp. olive oil

2 tbsp. unsalted butter, room temperature

1 tsp. minced garlic

1 tsp. fresh thyme leaves

Seafood

Air-Fried Catfish

Air-Fried Salmon with Tomato
Pan Sauce

Flounder with a Brown Butter
Piccata Sauce

Salmon with Spicy Black Bean Salsa

Air-Fried Shrimp

Pecan-Crusted Lemonfish with Lemon
Butter Sauce & Pecan Crab Relish

Emeril's Fish in a Pouch

Teriyaki-Glazed Cod

Air-Fried Catfish

DIRECTIONS

1. Combine the Creole seasoning and buttermilk in a small bowl and stir to combine. Add the fish fillets and turn to coat evenly.

2. Add the flour, cornmeal, salt, and black pepper to a separate bowl and stir to combine. Dredge the fillets in the cornmeal mixture, turning to coat evenly, and then transfer to a plate. Drizzle the fillets with the vegetable oil, turning to coat evenly.

3. Place the catfish on the Crisper Tray. Slide the Crisper Tray into Shelf Position 2. Select the Airfry setting (400° F/205° C). Set the cooking time to 10 mins. Press the Start Button to begin the cooking cycle.

4. Serve the catfish with the tartar sauce and lemons.

INGREDIENTS

1 ½ tsp. Creole seasoning (see p. 25)

½ cup buttermilk

½–¾ lb catfish fillets, cut into 2-in. strips if the fillets are large

½ cup all-purpose flour

⅓ cup cornmeal

1 tsp. salt

½ tsp. ground black pepper

2 tbsp. vegetable oil

lemon wedges, for serving

tartar sauce, for serving

Air-Fried Salmon
with Tomato Pan Sauce

INGREDIENTS

2 tbsp. olive oil, divided

2 6-oz salmon fillets, skin on (about 1-in thick)

1 ¼ tsp. kosher salt, divided

½ tsp. ground black pepper, divided

1 tbsp. minced shallot

1 tsp. minced garlic

1 vine-ripe tomato, diced

2 tbsp. tomato purée

3 tbsp. white wine vinegar

DIRECTIONS

1. Rub 1 tbsp. olive oil over the salmon and season with ¾ tsp. salt and ¼ tsp. black pepper.

2. Place the salmon on the Crisper Tray (skin side down). Slide the Crisper Tray into Shelf Position 2. Select the Airfry setting (400° F/205° C). Set the cooking time to 12 mins. Press the Start Button to begin the cooking cycle.

3. While the salmon cooks, place a small sauté pan on the stove top. Add the rest of the olive oil to the pan and heat the oil over medium-high heat. Once the oil is hot, add the shallot and garlic and stir until fragrant (about 30 secs.).

4. Add the tomato, tomato purée, white wine vinegar, and the rest of the salt and black pepper to the pan and cook until the sauce has reduced and begins to thicken (2–3 mins.).

5. When the cooking time is complete, remove the salmon from the Power AirFryer 360. Divide the sauce between two plates and serve the salmon on top of the sauce.

Flounder

with a Brown Butter Piccata Sauce

DIRECTIONS

1. Drizzle the olive oil over the flounder fillets and rub so that they are evenly coated on all sides. Then, season the fillets lightly with the salt and black pepper.

2. Arrange half of the lemon slices on the Baking Pan and place the fillets on top of the lemon slices. Slide the Pizza Rack into Shelf Position 1. Place the Baking Pan on top of the Pizza Rack. Select the Airfry setting (400° F/205° C). Set the cooking time to 8 mins. Press the Start Button to begin the cooking cycle. Cook until the fish is opaque and flakes easily (6–8 mins. for thin fillets or longer for thicker fillets).

3. Place a medium-size skillet on the stove top. Heat the skillet over medium-high heat until hot. Then, add the butter and let it melt, undisturbed, until it foams and turns a golden-brown color around the edges and smells fragrant and nutty. Swirl the pan and then add the lemon juice and capers. Season the sauce to taste with the salt and pepper black and then add the parsley.

4. Drizzle the sauce over the fillets when served.

INGREDIENTS

1 tbsp. extra virgin olive oil

4 4–6-oz skinless flounder fillets or other mild, white-flesh fish fillets such as cod, snapper, or drum

salt, to taste, divided

freshly ground black pepper, to taste, divided

1 ½ lemons, thinly sliced, divided

½ cup butter, cubed

juice of ½ lemon

2 tbsp. nonpareil capers, drained

1 tbsp. chopped parsley

Salmon
with Spicy Black Bean Salsa

DIRECTIONS

1. Combine the beans, tomatoes, red onion, bell pepper, jalapeño, cilantro, lime juice, and ¼ cup plus 1 tbsp. olive oil in a nonreactive bowl and stir to combine. Season the salsa with the salt and black pepper. Reserve the salsa while the salmon cooks.

2. Brush the salmon fillets with the rest of the olive oil and season on all sides with the salt and black pepper.

3. Place the salmon in the Crisper Tray (skin side down). Slide the Crisper Tray into Shelf Position 2. Select the Airfry setting (400° F/205° C). Set the cooking time to 12 mins. Press the Start Button to begin the cooking cycle.

4. When the salmon is done cooking, remove it from the Power AirFryer 360 and let rest briefly. Then, serve it with the salsa spooned over the top.

INGREDIENTS

1 15 ½-oz can black beans, drained & rinsed

2 medium vine-ripened tomatoes, cored, seeded & diced small

⅓ cup finely chopped red onion

⅓ cup finely chopped red bell pepper

1 jalapeño, minced (with seeds)

2 tbsp. coarsely chopped fresh cilantro

3 tbsp. lime juice

¼ cup plus 2 tbsp. olive oil, divided

kosher salt, to taste, divided

freshly ground black pepper, to taste, divided

4 6-oz portions salmon fillet, skin on

Air-Fried Shrimp

INGREDIENTS

12 oz medium or large shrimp, peeled & deveined

¼ tsp. salt

¼ tsp. ground black pepper

4 tsp. lemon juice

½ cup buttermilk

2 cups panko breadcrumbs

4 tbsp. vegetable oil

lemon wedges, for serving

cocktail sauce, for serving

DIRECTIONS

1. Season the shrimp with the salt and black pepper and place the shrimp in a small bowl. Add the lemon juice and toss to combine. Let the shrimp sit for 2 mins.

2. Add the buttermilk to the shrimp and stir to combine.

3. Select the Airfry setting (400° F/205° C). Set the cooking time to 6 mins. Press the Start Button and let the Power AirFryer 360 preheat.

4. Place the panko breadcrumbs in a small bowl. Dredge the shrimp in the breadcrumbs and toss to combine.

5. Transfer the shrimp to the Crisper Tray. Drizzle the vegetable oil over the shrimp and turn to coat evenly. Slide the Crisper Tray into Shelf Position 2. Cook until the shrimp are opaque and just cooked through.

6. Serve with the lemon wedges and cocktail sauce.

Pecan-Crusted Lemonfish

with Lemon Butter Sauce & Pecan Crab Relish

DIRECTIONS

1. Place a large nonreactive skillet on the stove top. Heat the skillet over high heat. Add the wine, lemons, garlic, and shallots and cook for 3 mins. while breaking up and mashing the lemons with a wire whisk. Stir in the salt, black pepper, Worcestershire sauce, and hot sauce and cook until the mixture is somewhat syrupy (about 3 mins.). Then, stir in the cream and cook for 1 min. Lower the heat to low and whisk in the butter a few pats at a time.

2. When all the butter has been added, remove the skillet from the heat while continuing to whisk until all the butter is incorporated into the sauce. Then, strain the sauce, pressing all the liquid into a bowl, and stir in the parsley. Keep warm until ready to use.

3. Combine the Pecan Crab Relish ingredients in a bowl and toss gently to keep from breaking up the crabmeat lumps. Refrigerate until ready to serve (up to 24 hrs.).

4. Select the Airfry setting (400° F/205° C). Set the cooking time to 15 mins. Press the Start Button and let the Power AirFryer 360 preheat.

5. Sprinkle ¾ tsp. Creole seasoning on each fillet and rub the seasoning on. Combine 1 cup flour and 1 tbsp. Creole seasoning in a bowl. Combine the pecans and the rest of the flour and Creole seasoning in a second bowl. Beat the eggs and milk together in a third bowl. Dredge the seasoned fillets first in the seasoned flour, then the egg wash, and finally the pecan–flour mixture. Gently shake off any excess.

6. When the Power AirFryer 360 has preheated, place the lemonfish on the Crisper Tray. Slide the Crisper Tray into Shelf Position 2.

7. When the cooking time is complete, top the lemonfish with the Pecan Crab Relish and serve with the lemon butter sauce.

INGREDIENTS

Lemon Butter Sauce

1 cup dry white wine

3 lemons, peeled & quartered

2 tbsp. minced garlic

1 tbsp. minced shallots

1 tsp. salt

3 turns freshly ground black pepper

1 dash Worcestershire sauce

1 dash hot pepper sauce

½ cup heavy cream

½ lb unsalted butter, cut into pieces, room temperature

1 tbsp. finely chopped fresh parsley

Pecan Crab Relish

1 cup lump crabmeat, picked over for shells & cartilage

½ cup roasted pecan halves

¼ cup chopped scallions

2 tbsp. minced red bell peppers

1 tsp. freshly squeezed lemon juice

½ tsp. salt

3 turns freshly ground black pepper

Lemonfish

3 tbsp. Creole seasoning (see p. 25)

4 6 oz lemonfish fillets

2 cups all-purpose flour

1 cup ground pecans

2 large eggs

1 cup milk

½ cup olive oil

Emeril's Fish in a Pouch

DIRECTIONS

1. Lay four 12-in. pieces of aluminum foil on a flat surface and drizzle each piece with 1 tbsp. olive oil. Sprinkle each fillet lightly with the Creole seasoning and place one fillet in the middle of each sheet.

2. Top each fillet with 2 tbsp. white wine, one quarter of the onions, and one quarter of the tomatoes. Sprinkle each fillet with the salt and black pepper, 1 tsp. garlic, and 1 tsp. basil and drizzle each fillet with 1 tsp. olive oil.

3. Bring two sides of each foil sheet up over the fillet and fold or crimp to seal. Fold the opposite edges to completely seal the pouches.

4. Transfer two pouches to the Pizza Rack. Slide the Pizza Rack into Shelf Position 5. Select the Bake setting. Set the cooking temperature to 375° F/190° C and set the cooking time to 20 mins. Press the Start Button to begin the cooking cycle. When the first batch is done cooking, remove the cooked pouches. Repeat the cooking process with the rest of the pouches.

5. When the cooking time is complete, carefully transfer the pouches to plates, slit the top of each pouch with scissors, and fold back the foil. Serve the fillets steaming hot in the packages or transfer to a plate or platter.

INGREDIENTS

5 tbsp. plus 1 tsp. olive oil, divided

4 6-oz fish fillets, such as pompano, scrod, snapper, flounder, grouper, haddock, tile, or sole

Creole seasoning, to taste

½ cup dry white wine (such as vinho verde)

2 large yellow onions, thinly sliced

8 Italian plum tomatoes, diced

salt, to taste

ground black pepper, to taste

1 tbsp. minced garlic

¼ cup chopped fresh basil

Teriyaki-Glazed Cod

DIRECTIONS

1. Place a small saucepan on the stove top. Combine the mirin, soy sauce, sugar, ginger, and garlic in the saucepan and bring to a boil. Then, lower the heat and simmer until reduced a thick glaze (5–6 mins.). Then, remove the saucepan from the heat. Reserve ¼ cup of the teriyaki sauce.

2. Set the cod fillets in a baking dish or a resealable plastic bag and toss with the unreserved teriyaki sauce. Marinate for at least 1 hr. in the refrigerator (up to overnight).

3. When ready to cook, transfer the cod to the Crisper Tray. Slide the Crisper Tray into Shelf Position 2. Select the Airfry setting (400° F/205° C). Set the cooking time to 12 mins. Press the Start Button to begin the cooking cycle.

4. When the cooking time is complete, carefully transfer the cod to four serving plates. Garnish the plates with the sesame seeds, scallions, and the rest of the glaze. Serve with your favorite vegetable or side dish.

INGREDIENTS

⅓ cup mirin

½ cup soy sauce

1 tbsp. sugar

2 tsp. minced ginger

1 tsp. minced garlic

4 6-oz cod fillets

¼ cup toasted sesame seeds

¼ cup thinly sliced scallions, green parts only

Family-Style Meals

Bacon & Corn Pudding

Mac & Cheese

Layered Chicken Enchiladas

Cheese Enchiladas with a Smoky
Red Chile Sauce

Jumbo Shells Stuffed with Ricotta,
Mushrooms & Roasted Red Peppers

Baked Cavatappi with Chicken
in a Pesto Cream Sauce

Chicken Sauce Piquante

Slow-Cooked Lasagna

Chuck Wagon Chili

Chicken Pot Pie

Bacon & Corn Pudding

DIRECTIONS

1. Place a medium-size sauté pan on the stove top and heat the pan over medium heat. When the pan is heated, add the bacon and cook while stirring as needed until most of the fat has rendered (3–4 mins.).

2. Add the corn, onion, bell pepper, celery, salt, Creole seasoning, and ground cayenne pepper to the pan and cook until softened (about 5 mins.). Then, add the garlic and thyme and remove the pan from the heat.

3. Add the milk, cream, and eggs to a medium-size bowl and whisk to combine. Fold in the bread, Monterey Jack, and the onion mixture. Set aside for 5 mins. to allow the bread to absorb some of the liquid.

4. Grease a 9 x 9 3-qt. casserole dish with the butter and transfer the pudding mixture to the pan.

5. Slide the Pizza Rack into Shelf Position 6. Place the casserole dish on the Pizza Rack. Select the Bake setting (325° F/165° C). Set the cooking time to 20 mins. Press the Start Button to begin the cooking cycle.

6. When the cooking time is complete, sprinkle the Parmesan evenly over the pudding.

7. Select the Bake setting. Set the cooking temperature to 300° F/149° C and set the cooking time to 10 mins. Press the Start Button to begin the cooking cycle.

8. When the cooking time is complete, remove the pudding from the Power AirFryer 360 and let cool for at least 30 mins. before serving.

INGREDIENTS

4 strips bacon, cut into ½-in. pieces

kernels from 2 ears corn (1 ½–2 cups)

¾ cup small-diced onion

½ cup small-diced red bell pepper

¼ cup small-diced celery

1 tsp. kosher salt

¾ tsp. Creole seasoning (see p. 25)

¼ tsp. ground cayenne pepper

2 tsp. minced garlic

1 tsp. fresh thyme leaves

1 ½ cups whole milk

½ cup heavy cream

3 large eggs

3 cups cubed day-old bread

1 cup grated Monterey Jack (about 4 oz)

1 tbsp. butter, softened

3 tbsp. finely grated Parmesan

Mac & Cheese

INGREDIENTS

2 tbsp. plus ½ tsp. salt, divided

1 lb elbow pasta (or your favorite pasta shape)

1 ½ cups whole milk

1 ½ cups heavy cream

1 cup grated Fontina

1 cup grated Gruyère

1 cup grated sharp cheddar

1 tsp. Creole seasoning (see p. 25)

½ tsp. ground black pepper

¼ tsp. ground nutmeg

½ cup breadcrumbs

½ cup finely grated Parmesan

2 tbsp. unsalted butter, melted

DIRECTIONS

1. Place a large saucepan on the stove top. Fill the saucepan three quarters full with water and bring to a boil over high heat. Once boiling, add 2 tbsp. salt and then the pasta to the water. Cook the pasta until just al dente according to the manufacturer's instructions.

2. Once the pasta is cooked, remove it from the water, drain well, and transfer it to a medium-size bowl. Add the milk, cream, Fontina, Gruyère, cheddar, Creole seasoning, black pepper, nutmeg, and ½ tsp. salt and stir well to combine. Then, transfer the pasta to a 9 ½ x 9 ½ baking dish and cover the dish with aluminum foil.

3. Slide the Pizza Rack into Shelf Position 6. Place the baking dish on the Pizza Rack. Select the Bake setting (325° F/165° C). Set the cooking time to 15 mins. Press the Start Button to begin the cooking cycle.

4. Combine the breadcrumbs, Parmesan, and butter in a small bowl and stir to blend. When the cooking time is complete, remove the foil and sprinkle the breadcrumb mixture over the pasta.

5. Select the Bake setting (325° F/165° C). Set the cooking time to 12 mins. Press the Start Button to begin the cooking cycle. Cook until the breadcrumbs are golden brown.

6. Let the mac and cheese cool for at least 20 mins. before serving.

Layered Chicken Enchiladas

DIRECTIONS

1. Place a 2-qt. or larger pot on the stove top. Heat the oil over medium-high heat. Then, stir in the flour and cook for 1 min.

2. Stir in the chili powder, oregano, cumin, and salt and cook for 30 secs.

3. Stir in the broth and tomato sauce and bring to a boil. Then, reduce the heat to low and simmer until the flavors are blended (about 15 mins.). Once done, set the enchilada sauce aside to cool.

4. Combine the chicken with the cheddar, Monterey Jack, and onion in a medium-size bowl.

5. Add 1 cup enchilada sauce to a 4 ½-qt. oval casserole dish and top with 4 tortillas (they will overlap slightly). Add 2 cups of the chicken and cheese filling, spreading evenly, and then top with another 4 tortillas. Continue to build two more layers of the sauce, filling, and tortillas. Top the final layer with 1 cup of the sauce.

6. Slide the Pizza Rack into Shelf Position 6. Place the casserole dish on the Pizza Rack. Select the Slow Cook setting. Set the cooking temperature to 250° F/121° C and the cooking time to 2 hrs. Press the Start Button to begin the cooking cycle. During the last 10 mins. of cooking, top the enchiladas with ½ cup of sauce.

7. Before serving, garnish the enchiladas with the cotija cheese, cilantro, and scallion and let sit for 10 mins.

8. To serve, cut the enchiladas into desired portions and serve with additional sauce and the sour cream.

INGREDIENTS

¼ cup plus 2 tbsp. vegetable oil

¼ cup plus 2 tbsp. flour

½ cup chili powder (about 2 oz)

2 tsp. dried oregano

1 tsp. ground cumin

½ tsp. salt

1 qt. chicken broth

2 15-oz cans tomato sauce

4 cups shredded or diced cooked chicken

½ lb shredded cheddar

¼ lb shredded Monterey Jack

1 cup chopped onion

16 6-in. corn tortillas

¾ cup crumbled cotija cheese, for garnish

½ cup chopped fresh cilantro leaves, for garnish

1 cup chopped scallion, for garnish

sour cream, for serving

Cheese Enchiladas
with a Smoky Red Chile Sauce

DIRECTIONS

1. Place a small saucepot on the stove top. Bring the water to a boil in the saucepot. Then, remove the saucepot from the heat, cover, and reserve.

2. Place a 12-in. sauté pan on the stove top. Heat the pan over medium heat. Toast the garlic on one side of the pan and cook while turning frequently until dark spots appear on the skin and the garlic softens inside its peel (about 15 mins.). Remove the garlic from the pan, peel, and reserve.

3. While the garlic is toasting, toast the dried chiles on the other side of the pan while flattening and pressing the chiles down with a spatula until the oils are released (2–3 mins. per side). Transfer the chiles to the pot of hot water and weight them to keep them submerged. Cover and soak until the chiles are reconstituted (2–3 hrs.).

4. Wipe the pan clean with a paper towel. Heat 2 tbsp. olive oil over medium-high heat. Add the onions and ¼ tsp. salt and cook until the onions are lightly caramelized and tender (about 5 mins.). Add the garlic, thyme, oregano, and cinnamon and cook until fragrant (about 30 secs.). Add the tomatoes and 2 cups stock and bring to a boil. Then, reduce the heat and simmer until the flavors come together (about 4 mins.). Add the rest of the salt and black pepper, stir , and reserve. Discard the cinnamon.

5. Transfer the chiles to a blender and add ½ cup of the soaking water and blend until puréed. Then, strain the chiles through a fine mesh sieve, pressing to extract as much of the chiles as possible. Discard the solids. Return the puréed chiles to the blender and add the onion–tomato mixture and the rest of the stock. Place a towel on top of the blender (use caution when blending hot liquids) and purée until smooth.

6. Clean the sauté pan. Add 3 tbsp. olive oil and heat the oil over medium-high heat. Add a tortilla and cook until soft and pliable (about 20 secs. per side), allowing any excess oil to drip into the pan. Then, transfer the tortilla to a paper towel-lined baking sheet. Repeat with the rest of the tortillas, adding the rest of the oil as needed.

7. Lightly season the tortillas with salt. Place 2 tbsp. pepper jack and 1 tbsp. cotija cheese down the center of each tortilla. Roll the tortillas up and place them seam side down in a 9 ½ x 9 ½ baking dish. Pour the sauce over the tortillas and sprinkle the queso blanco over the sauce.

8. Slide the Pizza Rack into Shelf Position 6. Place the baking dish on the Pizza Rack. Select the Bake setting (325° F/165° C). Set the cooking time to 15 mins. Press the Start Button to begin the cooking cycle. When the cooking time is complete, remove the enchiladas from the oven, sprinkle with the cilantro, and serve immediately.

INGREDIENTS

6 cups water

2 large garlic cloves, unpeeled

½ oz dried guajillo chiles (about 5 chiles), seeded & deveined

½ oz dried ancho chiles (about 5 chiles), seeded & deveined

¼ cup olive oil, divided

½ cup small-diced onions

½ tsp. salt, plus more for seasoning

½ tsp. dried thyme, crushed between your fingers

½ tsp. dried Mexican oregano, crushed between your fingers

½ cinnamon stick

½ 14 ½-oz can diced tomatoes, drained

1 ¼ cups chicken stock or canned low-sodium chicken broth, divided

½ tsp. freshly ground black pepper

6 corn tortillas

6 oz pepper jack, shredded

4 oz finely shredded cotija cheese

1 oz finely shredded queso blanco

1 tbsp. roughly chopped cilantro leaves

Jumbo Shells

Stuffed with Ricotta, Mushrooms & Roasted Red Peppers

INGREDIENTS

24–30 jumbo shells

¼ cup extra virgin olive oil, divided

¼ cup plus 2 tbsp. butter

1 cup chopped onions

2 tbsp. minced garlic, divided

1 lb mixed mushrooms, such as button & shiitake, destemmed, cleaned & thinly sliced

¼ cup sweet marsala wine

1 ½ tsp. salt, divided

1 tsp. freshly ground black pepper, divided

2 ½ cups whole milk ricotta

1 lb jarred roasted red peppers, drained well & chopped finely

¾ cup chopped mixed fresh soft herb leaves, such as parsley, basil, oregano, marjoram & thyme

1 egg, beaten lightly

3 cups homemade marinara sauce

¾ lb grated mozzarella

½ cup grated Parmigiano-Reggiano

DIRECTIONS

1. Place a 4–6-qt. pot on the stove top. Fill the pot with salted water and bring to a boil over high heat. Add the shells to the pot and cook until al dente (about 12 mins.). Then, use a slotted spoon to transfer the shells gently to a baking sheet. Drizzle 2 tbsp. olive oil over the shells to prevent them from sticking to one another and set them aside to cool.

2. Place a 10-in. skillet on the stove top. Melt the butter over medium-high heat. Then, add the onions and cook while stirring as needed until translucent and soft (about 2 mins.). Add 1 tbsp. garlic and cook for 1 min.

3. Increase the heat to high, add the mushrooms, and cook until nicely browned and the liquid has evaporated (about 4 mins.). Add the marsala, ½ tsp. salt, and ½ tsp. black pepper. Cook until the liquid is absorbed (about 1 min.). Remove the mushrooms from the heat and set aside.

4. Combine the ricotta, red peppers, herbs, mushrooms, egg, and the rest of the olive oil, garlic, salt, black pepper and stir well to combine.

5. Place 2 tbsp. of the stuffing into each of the 24 nicest shells (a few may have broken during cooking), and place them, open-end down, in a 9 x 9 3-qt. casserole dish. Any extra filling may be placed in any extra shells that are available. Pour the marinara sauce evenly over the shells and top with the grated mozzarella and Parmesan.

6. Slide the Pizza Rack into Shelf Position 6. Place the casserole dish on the Pizza Rack. Select the Bake setting (325° F/165° C). Set the cooking time to 20 mins. Press the Start Button to begin the cooking cycle.

7. When the cooking time is complete, remove the dish and serve the shells hot.

Baked Cavatappi

with Chicken in a Pesto Cream Sauce

DIRECTIONS

1. Cook the pasta in a large pot of salted water until just under al dente (2–3 mins. less than the package's cooking instructions). Drain the pasta, drizzle with 1 tbsp. olive oil, and toss to coat. Reserve the pasta.

2. Place a 12-in. sauté pan on the stove top. Heat 1 tbsp. olive oil over medium heat. Add the chicken, ¼ tsp. salt, and ¼ tsp. black pepper stir until opaque (about 2 mins.). Remove and reserve the chicken.

3. Add the onions and 1 tbsp. olive oil to the pan and cook until tender (about 4 mins.). Add 1 tsp. garlic and cook until fragrant (about 20 secs.). Add the spinach and ¼ tsp. salt and cook until the spinach begins to wilt (1–2 mins.). Remove and reserve the mixture.

4. Combine the red pepper, pine nuts, ¼ tsp. lemon zest, and 1 tsp. garlic in a food processor and pulse until blended. Scrape down the sides. Add the basil, ½ cup olive oil, ¼ tsp. salt, and ¼ tsp. black pepper and pulse until completely blended to make pesto. Reserve the pesto.

5. Wipe the sauté pan clean. Return the pan to the stove top over medium heat. Add the butter and flour and whisk. Cook while whisking constantly for about 2 mins. (do not let the flour brown). Then, whisk in 2 ½ cups of milk, ½ cup at a time, and cook until thickened (4–6 mins.). Remove the pan from the heat and stir in the pesto, 1 tsp. salt, ¼ tsp. black pepper, and 6 oz Parmigiano-Reggiano.

6. Grease a 9 x 9 3-qt. casserole dish with 1 tbsp. olive oil. Combine the pasta, chicken, spinach mixture, pesto sauce, and 1 tsp. lemon zest in a mixing bowl and toss to mix well. Pour the mixture into the dish. Sprinkle the top of the mixture with 2 oz Parmigiano-Reggiano.

7. Slide the Pizza Rack into Shelf Position 6. Place the baking dish on the Pizza Rack. Select the Bake setting (30-min. cooking time). Set the cooking temperature to 300° F/149° C. Press the Start Button to begin the cooking cycle. When the cooking time is complete, serve with salad.

INGREDIENTS

1 lb dried cavatappi pasta

1 ¾ tsp. salt, plus more for cooking pasta, divided

¾ cup olive oil, divided

1 lb boneless & skinless chicken breast, thinly sliced

¾ tsp. freshly ground black pepper, divided

1 cup small-diced onions

2 tsp. minced garlic, divided

9 oz spinach, washed, tough stems removed, chopped roughly

¼ tsp. crushed red pepper

½ cup toasted pine nuts

1 ¼ tsp. finely grated lemon zest, divided

1 cup packed fresh basil leaves

3 tbsp. unsalted butter

3 tbsp. all-purpose flour

3 ½ cups whole milk

8 oz finely grated Parmigiano-Reggiano, divided

Chicken Sauce Piquante

DIRECTIONS

1. Add the chicken pieces to a large mixing bowl and season all over with the Creole seasoning. Add the flour and mix well until the chicken is evenly coated. Shake the chicken to remove any excess flour and then reserve the chicken on a plate.

2. Place a 12-in. or larger skillet on the stove top. Heat the vegetable oil over medium-high heat. Then, add the chicken pieces to the pan (in batches if necessary) and cook until golden brown on all sides (about 8 mins.). Transfer the browned chicken pieces to a 4 ½-qt. Dutch oven.

3. Add the onion, bell pepper, celery, and jalapeño to the skillet and cook for 2 mins., stirring to incorporate the browned bits from the bottom of the pan.

4. Add the garlic, crushed red pepper, thyme, ground cayenne pepper, and bay leaves and cook for 1 min.

5. Add the tomatoes (breaking them up into pieces with the spoon), tomato paste, Worcestershire sauce, sugar, and salt. Then, add ½ cup of the reserved tomato juice, bring to a simmer, and cook for 1 min. Transfer the hot sauce to the Dutch oven. Cover the Dutch oven.

6. Slide the Pizza Rack into Shelf Position 6. Place the Dutch oven on the Pizza Rack. Select the Slow Cook setting (225° F/107° C). Set the cooking time to 2 ½ hrs. Press the Start Button to begin the cooking cycle.

7. Once the cooking time is complete, add the parsley to the chicken sauce piquante and serve over the steamed rice.

INGREDIENTS

1 4-lb chicken, cut into 8 pieces

1 tbsp. Creole seasoning (see p. 25)

½ cup flour

3 tbsp. vegetable oil

1 medium onion, chopped (about 1 cup)

1 medium green bell pepper, chopped (about 1 cup)

¾ cup chopped celery, leaves okay

½ jalapeño, chopped

1 ½ tsp. chopped garlic

½ tsp. crushed red pepper

½ tsp. dried thyme

¼ tsp. ground cayenne pepper

2 bay leaves

1 28-oz can whole tomatoes, drained & juice reserved

¼ cup tomato paste

1 tbsp. Worcestershire sauce

1 tsp. sugar

1 tsp. salt

¼ cup chopped fresh parsley leaves

steamed white rice, for serving

Slow-Cooked Lasagna

DIRECTIONS

1. Place a 12–14-in. skillet on the stove top and heat the skillet over medium-high heat. Add the beef, veal, and pork and cook while stirring as needed until browned (about 8 mins.).

2. Add the celery, onion, and garlic and cook for 2 mins.

3. Stir in the tomatoes, broth, salt, black pepper, crushed red pepper, oregano, basil, thyme, and sugar and simmer for 5 mins. Then, remove the skillet from the heat and set aside to cool. The meat sauce can be made up to several days in advance (it freezes well too).

4. Combine the ricotta and the egg in a medium-size bowl. Then, stir in ½ cup of the cooled meat sauce.

5. Add ½ cup of the meat sauce to a 4 ½-qt. Dutch oven. Top the sauce with 3 lasagna noodles, side by side. Place 6 heaping tbsp. of the ricotta mixture on the noodles and spread evenly. Top the noodles with one third of the grated mozzarella, one third of the provolone, and one third of the fresh mozzarella. Top with 2 cups of the meat sauce. Make two more layers without adding a layer of cheese to the final set of layers.

6. Slide the Pizza Rack into Shelf Position 6. Place the Dutch oven on the Pizza Rack. Select the Slow Cook setting (225° F/107° C). Set the cooking time to 4 hrs. Press the Start Button to begin the cooking cycle. Cover the Dutch oven.

7. When the cooking time is complete, top the lasagna with the Parmigiano-Reggiano and the rest of the grated mozzarella, provolone, and fresh mozzarella and close the lid. Allow the cheese to melt and the lasagna to set by cooling for at least 30 mins. before serving.

INGREDIENTS

Meat Sauce

⅓ lb ground beef

⅓ lb ground veal

⅓ lb ground pork

½ cup chopped celery

½ cup chopped onion

3 tbsp. chopped garlic

2 28-oz cans crushed tomatoes

1 cup beef broth

1 tbsp. salt

1 ½ tsp. freshly ground black pepper

½ tsp. crushed red pepper

1 tsp. dried oregano

1 tsp. dried basil

1 tsp. dried thyme

1 ½ tsp. sugar

Lasagna

1 15-oz container ricotta

1 egg

9 dried lasagna noodles, ends broken to fit in a 4 ½-qt. Dutch oven

¾ lb grated mozzarella, divided

½ lb sliced provolone, divided

½ lb fresh mozzarella, sliced, divided

⅓ cup finely grated Parmigiano-Reggiano

Chuck Wagon Chili

DIRECTIONS

1. Combine the chili powder, cumin seeds, ground cayenne pepper, cinnamon, oregano, bay leaves, and brown sugar in a small bowl. Reserve the spice mixture.

2. Add the beef to a medium-size bowl and season with the black pepper and 1 tbsp. salt.

3. Place a 12-in. skillet on the stove top. Heat 2 tbsp. vegetable oil over high heat. Then, add enough beef to fill the pan and cook until nicely browned on one side (about 2 mins.). Turn the pieces over and cook for another 2 mins.

4. Transfer the browned beef to the crock of a 4 ½-qt. Dutch Oven. Add the onions, celery, and 1 tbsp. salt to the skillet and cook while stirring until the vegetables begin to soften (about 2 mins.).

5. Add the garlic, jalapeños, and spice mixture and cook for 1 min. Then, pour in the beer, tomato paste, and crushed tomatoes and simmer for 3 mins.

6. Stir in the chocolate, masa harina, and the rest of the salt and cook for 1 min. Transfer this mixture to the Dutch Oven and cover.

7. Slide the Pizza Rack into Shelf Position 6. Place the Dutch Oven on the Pizza Rack. Select the Slow Cook setting (4-hr. cook time). Set the cooking temperature to 275° F/135° C. Press the Start Button to begin the cooking cycle.

8. When the cooking time is complete, remove the bay leaves and stir in the cilantro and parsley. Serve the chili hot in bowls and top the chili with the grated cheddar, chopped scallions, and sour cream.

INGREDIENTS

¼ cup chili powder

2 tbsp. whole cumin seeds

1 tsp. ground cayenne pepper

¾ tsp. ground cinnamon

2 tsp. dried Mexican or regular oregano, crumbled between your fingers

3 bay leaves

2 tsp. light or dark brown sugar

4 lb boneless beef chuck, trimmed and cut into 1 ½–2-in. cubes

1 tsp. freshly ground black pepper

2 ½ tbsp. kosher salt, divided

3 tbsp. vegetable oil, divided

3 medium-size onions, coarsely chopped (about 4 cups)

1 ½ cups chopped celery, including leaves

6 cloves garlic, roughly chopped

2 jalapeños, roughly chopped

12 oz dark Mexican beer

2 tbsp. tomato paste

28 oz crushed tomatoes

1 oz semisweet chocolate, coarsely chopped

3 tbsp. masa harina (corn flour, not cornstarch)

½ cup chopped fresh cilantro leaves

½ cup chopped fresh parsley leaves

grated cheddar, for garnish

chopped scallions, for garnish

sour cream, for garnish

Chicken Pot Pie

DIRECTIONS

1. Place a 3-qt. pot on the stove top. Melt the butter over medium heat. Then, sauté the mushrooms, onions, carrots, celery, and garlic (about 3 mins.).

2. Add the salt, black pepper, and 6 tbsp. flour and cook while stirring for about 2 mins.

3. Add the chicken and cook for about 5 mins.

4. Add the broth, stir, and simmer for about 20 mins. Then, remove from the heat and add the peas and parsley.

5. Dust a work surface with flour and roll out the puff pastry over the flour. Invert a 9 x 9 3-qt. casserole dish over the puff pastry and use a small knife to cut around the casserole dish 1 in. wider than the casserole dish.

6. Fill the casserole dish with the filling. Place the puff pastry on top of the casserole dish loosely. Cut a small hole in the center of the pastry for a vent hole.

7. Whisk the egg together with 1 tbsp. water in a small bowl to make egg wash. Paint the puff pastry with the egg wash.

8. Slide the Pizza Rack into Shelf Position 5. Place the casserole dish on the Pizza Rack. Select the Airfry setting (400° F/205° C). Set the cooking time to 20 mins. Press the Start Button to begin the cooking cycle. Cook until the puff pastry has puffed and is golden brown.

9. When the cooking time is complete, serve immediately.

INGREDIENTS

6 tbsp. butter

1 ½ cups chopped button mushrooms

1 ½ cups chopped onions

1 ½ cups chopped carrots

¾ cup chopped celery

1 tbsp. chopped garlic

1 tsp. kosher salt

1 tsp. freshly ground black pepper

6 tbsp. flour, plus more for dusting

2 lb boneless & skinless chicken thigh, cut into bite-size pieces

3 cups chicken broth

½ cup frozen green peas

4 ½ tsp. chopped parsley

1 sheet puff pastry, thawed

1 egg, whisked

Vegetables

French Fries with Paprika–Parmesan Salt

Herb-Roasted Baby Potatoes

Herb-Roasted Mushrooms

Cauliflower with Romesco

Green Beans with Shallots & Almonds

Asparagus with Choron Sauce

Baby Beets with Ricotta & Pistachios

Corn with Chili & Cheese

Air-Fried Squash with Goat Cheese,
Herbed Salsa & Pine Nuts

Roasted Cauliflower with Garlic
& Rosemary

Brussels Sprouts with Lemon, Garlic
& Parmesan

Double-Stuffed Potatoes

French Fries

with Paprika–Parmesan Salt

DIRECTIONS

1. Peel the potatoes and cut them lengthwise into ½ in.-thick slices. Turn each side flat and slice again lengthwise into even ½ in.-thick fries. Place the potatoes in a bowl and cover with cool water. Let them soak for at least 30 mins. (up to overnight).

2. Combine the Parmesan, paprika, garlic powder, onion powder, and salt in a small bowl and reserve.

3. Place the potatoes on the Crisper Tray. Slide the Crisper Tray into Shelf Position 2. Select the Airfry setting (400° F/205° C for 18 mins.). Press the Start Button to begin the cooking cycle.

4. When the cooking time is complete, stir the fries. Select the Airfry setting (400° F/205° C for 18 mins.). Press the Start Button to begin the cooking cycle.

5. When the cooking time is complete, sprinkle the fries with the Paprika–Parmesan salt.

INGREDIENTS

2 lb russet potatoes

2 tbsp. finely grated Parmesan

1 ½ tsp. paprika

¼ tsp. garlic powder

⅛ tsp. onion powder

¾ tsp. salt

2 tbsp. vegetable oil

Herb-Roasted Baby Potatoes

INGREDIENTS

2 lb assorted baby potatoes, halved

3 tbsp. olive oil

1 tsp. chopped fresh rosemary

1 tsp. chopped fresh oregano

1 tsp. chopped fresh thyme

1 tsp. kosher salt

½ tsp. freshly ground black pepper

DIRECTIONS

1. Combine all the ingredients in a large mixing bowl and toss.

2. Place the potatoes on the Crisper Tray. Slide the Crisper Tray into Shelf Position 2. Select the Airfry setting (400° F/205° C). Set the cooking time to 20 mins. Press the Start Button to begin the cooking cycle. Halfway through the cooking time (10 mins.), stir the potatoes.

3. When the cooking time is complete, transfer the potatoes to a platter and serve warm.

Herb-Roasted Mushrooms

DIRECTIONS

1. Combine all the ingredients in a bowl and toss.

2. Place the mushrooms on the Baking Pan. Slide the Pizza Rack into Shelf Position 2. Place the Baking Pan on top of the Pizza Rack. Select the Airfry setting (400° F/205° C). Set the cooking time to 8 mins. Press the Start Button to begin the cooking cycle.

3. When the cooking time is complete, serve immediately as a side to your favorite entrée.

INGREDIENTS

3 tbsp. butter, melted

2 sliced shallots

1 tbsp. minced garlic

2 lb assorted mushrooms, such as shiitake, cremini & enoki, thinly sliced

salt, to taste

ground black pepper, to taste

1 tbsp. fresh chopped thyme leaves

1 tbsp. fresh chopped marjoram leaves

INGREDIENTS

Romesco Sauce

1 large red pepper

1 tsp. olive oil

1 clove garlic, smashed

½ cup toasted slivered almonds

¼ cup tomato sauce

2 tbsp. chopped parsley

2 tbsp. chopped fresh basil or mint

2 tsp. chopped fresh oregano

2 tbsp. sherry vinegar

¾ tsp. ground cayenne pepper

⅔ cup extra virgin olive oil

salt, to taste

ground black pepper, to taste

———

1 2 ½-lb head cauliflower, stemmed & cut into 1 ½–2-in. florets

2 tbsp. olive oil

1 tsp. salt

½ tsp. ground white pepper

3 tbsp. golden raisins

2 tbsp. chopped nonpareil capers

Cauliflower with Romesco

DIRECTIONS

1. Rub the red pepper with 1 tsp. olive oil and place the pepper on the Baking Pan.

2. Slide the Pizza Rack into Shelf Position 5. Place the Baking Pan on top of the Pizza Rack. Select the Airfry setting (400° F/205° C). Set the cooking time to 15 mins. Press the Start Button to begin the cooking cycle. Turn the pepper occasionally while it is cooking and cook until the pepper is charred all over.

3. When the cooking time is complete, transfer the pepper to a plastic bag and peel and seed the pepper.

4. Place all the sauce ingredients in a food processor and blend until smooth.

5. Combine the cauliflower, olive oil, salt, and black pepper in a medium-size bowl and toss.

6. Place the cauliflower on the Crisper Tray. Slide the Crisper Tray into Shelf Position 5. Select the Airfry setting (400° F/205° C). Set the cooking time to 20 mins. Press the Start Button to begin the cooking cycle. After 15 mins., add the raisins.

7. When the cooking time is complete, transfer the cauliflower to a dish, sprinkle the cauliflower with the capers, and serve with the Romesco Sauce.

Green Beans

with Shallots & Almonds

DIRECTIONS

1. Place a large saucepan on the stove top. Fill the saucepan three quarters full with water and bring to a boil over high heat. Add the green beans and 1 tbsp. salt and cook for 2 mins. Remove the green beans from the water and drain in a colander.

2. Place the green beans in a large bowl and add the shallots, white pepper, olive oil, and the rest of the salt and toss well to coat evenly.

3. Place the green beans on the Crisper Tray. Slide the Crisper Tray into Shelf Position 2. Select the Airfry setting (18-min. cook time). Set the cooking temperature to 350° F/175° C. Press the Start Button to begin the cooking cycle. Stir the green beans every 6 mins. while they are cooking.

4. When the cooking time is complete, transfer the green beans to a bowl and toss them with the almonds.

INGREDIENTS

1 ½ lb French green beans, stems removed

1 tbsp. plus 1 tsp. salt, divided

½ lb shallots, peeled, stem end removed, cut into quarters

½ tsp. ground white pepper

2 tbsp. olive oil

¼ cup slivered almonds, toasted lightly

Asparagus with Choron Sauce

DIRECTIONS

1. Place a small saucepan on the stove top. Combine the white wine vinegar, shallots, peppercorns and 2 tbsp. tarragon leaves in the saucepan and bring to a boil over medium-high heat. Cook until reduced by two thirds (about 3 mins.).

2. Remove the saucepan from the heat and strain the sauce into a heatproof bowl. Add the egg yolks and water and whisk to incorporate. Set the bowl over a pan with simmering water on the stove top and continue to whisk until the egg starts to thicken (2–3 mins.).

3. Remove the bowl from the heat and slowly drizzle a little of the clarified butter into the bowl while whisking constantly to incorporate. Return the bowl to the heat, whisk, and when the egg starts to thicken again, continue to add more of the butter to the egg. Continue this on-the-heat, off-the-heat pattern until all the clarified butter is incorporated.

4. Season with the salt and white pepper, fold the tomatoes into the sauce, and add the rest of the tarragon. Keep the sauce warm while you cook the asparagus (do not allow the sauce to boil or it will separate).

5. Place the asparagus on the Crisper Tray. Slide the Crisper Tray into Shelf Position 2. Select the Airfry setting (400° F/205° C). Set the cooking time to 8 mins. Press the Start Button to begin the cooking cycle.

6. When the cooking time is complete, transfer the asparagus to a serving plate, ladle the sauce over the asparagus, and serve warm.

INGREDIENTS

⅓ cup white wine vinegar

1 tbsp. minced shallots

½ tsp. black peppercorns

3 tbsp. chopped tarragon leaves, divided

3 egg yolks

2 tsp. warm water

1 cup clarified butter

salt, to taste

ground white pepper, to taste

¼ cup seeded & diced tomatoes

1 lb asparagus, woody ends trimmed

Baby Beets
with Ricotta & Pistachios

DIRECTIONS

1. Combine the beets, olive oil, salt, and black pepper in a medium-size bowl and toss well.

2. Wrap the beets in foil and place them on the Crisper Tray. Slide the Crisper Tray into Shelf Position 2. Select the Airfry setting (400° F/205° C). Set the cooking time to 40 mins. Press the Start Button to begin the cooking cycle.

3. When the cooking time is complete, transfer the beets to a serving dish and sprinkle them with the tarragon, mint, and ricotta. Drizzle with the honey and then sprinkle the pistachios over everything.

INGREDIENTS

3 ½–4 lb baby beets, peeled & tops removed

2 tbsp. olive oil

1 tsp. kosher salt

½ tsp. ground black pepper

1 tsp. chopped fresh tarragon

1 tsp. chopped fresh mint

⅓ cup fresh ricotta

1 tbsp. honey, to taste

3 tbsp. chopped toasted pistachios

Corn with Chili & Cheese

DIRECTIONS

1. Combine the sour cream and milk in a small bowl. Reserve the sour cream mixture.

2. Cut the corn in half and brush the corn generously with the melted butter.

3. Place the corn on the Crisper Tray. Slide the Crisper Tray into Shelf Position 2. Select the Airfry setting (400° F/205° C). Set the cooking time to 8 mins. Press the Start Button to begin the cooking cycle. Cook until the corn is crisp-tender and lightly golden in places

4. When the cooking time is complete, transfer the corn to a platter and squeeze the lime over the cooked corn. Brush the ears with some of the sour cream mixture. Coat the corn evenly on all sides with the cheese, sprinkle the corn with the chili powder and kosher salt, and serve immediately.

INGREDIENTS

½ cup sour cream

2 tbsp. whole milk

4 ears fresh sweet corn, silk & husks removed

3 tbsp. butter, melted

1 lime, halved

½ cup finely grated queso añejo, queso fresco, or Parmesan

1 tbsp. chili powder

1 ½ tsp. kosher salt

Air-Fried Squash

with Goat Cheese, Herbed Salsa & Pine Nuts

INGREDIENTS

2 ½ lb summer squash, sliced crosswise into ½-in. pieces

2 tbsp. extra virgin olive oil, plus more for drizzling if desired, divided

1 ¼ tsp. kosher salt, divided

½ tsp. ground black pepper

1 ½ cups finely chopped ripe tomatoes

1 tbsp. champagne vinegar or white wine vinegar

¼ tsp. minced garlic

2 tbsp. chopped mixed fresh soft herbs, such as mint, basil & cilantro

2 oz soft crumbled goat cheese

3 tbsp. toasted pine nuts

DIRECTIONS

1. Combine the squash with 2 tbsp. olive oil, ¾ tsp. salt, and the black pepper in a large mixing bowl. Toss to evenly coat.

2. Place the squash on the Crisper Tray. Slide the Crisper Tray into Shelf Position 2. Select the Airfry setting (400° F/205° C). Set the cooking time to 20 mins. Press the Start Button to begin the cooking cycle.

3. While the squash is cooking, combine the tomatoes, vinegar, garlic, herbs, and ½ tsp. salt in a small bowl and stir to blend.

4. When the cooking time is complete, transfer the squash to a serving plate and sprinkle it with the goat cheese and pine nuts. Drizzle the herbed salsa over everything and serve either warm or at room temperature and drizzled with more olive oil if desired.

Roasted Cauliflower

with Garlic & Rosemary

DIRECTIONS

1. Combine all the ingredients in a bowl and toss.

2. Place the cauliflower on the Crisper Tray. Slide the Crisper Tray into Shelf Position 2. Select the Airfry setting (400° F/205° C for 18 mins.). Press the Start Button to begin the cooking cycle.

3. When the cooking time is complete, plate the cauliflower and serve.

INGREDIENTS

1 head cauliflower, trimmed & cut into medium-size florets

2 tbsp. extra virgin olive oil

2 cloves garlic, minced

1 ½ tsp. finely chopped fresh rosemary

¾ tsp. kosher salt

½ tsp. freshly ground black pepper

Brussels Sprouts

with Lemon, Garlic & Parmesan

DIRECTIONS

1. Toss the Brussels sprouts with the olive oil, salt, and crushed red pepper to coat evenly.

2. Place the Brussels sprouts on the Crisper Tray. Top the Brussels sprouts with the bacon. Slide the Crisper Tray into Shelf Position 2. Select the Airfry setting (400° F/205° C for 18 mins.). Press the Start Button to begin the cooking cycle. Halfway through the cooking time (9 mins.), stir the Brussels sprouts. Cook until the Brussels sprouts are crispy.

3. Transfer the Brussels sprouts to a bowl and toss with the garlic, lemon zest, and Parmesan. Serve hot or warm.

INGREDIENTS

2 lb Brussels sprouts, cleaned & halved

3 tbsp. olive oil

1 tsp. kosher salt

½ tsp. crushed red pepper

2 oz thick-cut bacon, sliced into ½ in. lengths

1 tsp. minced garlic

finely grated zest of ¼ lemon

3 tbsp. Parmesan

Double-Stuffed Potatoes

DIRECTIONS

1. Pierce each potato a couple times with a fork or paring knife. Place the potatoes on the Pizza Rack. Slide the Pizza Rack into Shelf Position 2. Select the Bake setting. Set the cooking temperature to 350° F/177° C and set the cooking time to 45 mins. Press the Start Button to begin the cooking cycle.

2. When the cooking time is complete, hold the potatoes with a towel and cut each potato in half to form a canoe. Carefully scoop the inside of the potatoes into a small bowl. Mash the potato with the tines of a fork. Add the sour cream, butter, bacon, scallions, salt, white pepper, and ½ cup cheddar and mix.

3. Refill the potatoes with the reserved insides of the potatoes and top with the rest of the cheddar.

4. Place the potatoes on the Crisper Tray. Slide the Crisper Tray into Shelf Position 2. Select the Airfry setting (400° F/205° C). Set the cooking time to 5 mins. Press the Start Button to begin the cooking cycle. Cook until the cheese is melted.

INGREDIENTS

2 russet potatoes

⅓ cup sour cream

½ stick unsalted butter

4 slices bacon, cooked

2 tbsp. chopped scallions

1 tsp. salt

½ tsp. ground white pepper

1 cup shredded cheddar, divided

Desserts

Layer Cake with Seven-Minute Frosting

Pecan Pie

Sweet Potato Pie

Peanut Butter & Chocolate Chip Cookies

Mixed Berry Crisp

Creole Bread Pudding with Bourbon Sauce

Lemon Poppy Seed Cake

Blueberry Pie

EMERIL LAGASSE

Layer Cake
with Seven-Minute Frosting

DIRECTIONS

1. Grease and flour two cake pans. Prepare the cake mix according to its packaging's instructions and then pour the batter into the prepared pans.

2. Select the Bake setting (325° F/165° C). Set the cooking time to 35 mins. Press the Start Button and let the Power AirFryer 360 preheat.

3. When the Power AirFryer 360 has preheated, slide the Pizza Rack into Shelf Position 5. Place one of the cake pans on the Pizza Rack. Cook until a toothpick inserted into the center of the cake comes out clean. When the cake is done, repeat the process with the second cake.

4. Allow the cakes to cool in the pan for at least 10 mins. before inverting on a wire rack to cool completely.

5. Place a small, heavy-bottomed saucepan on the stove top. Add the sugar, corn syrup, cream of tartar, salt, and water and whisk together. Bring the mixture to a boil over medium heat and cook, undisturbed (do not stir the mixture; stirring can cause the sugar to crystallize), until a candy thermometer inserted into the mixture reads 240° F/116° C (about 2 mins.).

6. While the mixture heats up, add the egg whites to a medium-size bowl. Use an electric mixer on high speed to beat the egg whites until foamy.

7. Once the sugar syrup reaches 240° F/116° C, immediately and carefully pour the syrup into the egg whites with the mixer running on high speed away from the beaters to prevent splattering and possible burns. Continue to beat until the frosting is glossy and fluffy (about 5 mins.). Then, beat in the almond or vanilla extract.

8. Frost the top of one cake half. Place the other cake half on top of the frosting and then frost the top of the cake.

INGREDIENTS

pan spray

flour, for dusting

1 box chocolate cake mix

Seven-Minute Frosting

1 cup sugar

2 tbsp. light corn syrup

½ tsp. cream of tartar

1 pinch salt

⅓ cup water

3 large egg whites, room temperature

1 tsp. almond or vanilla extract

Pecan Pie

DIRECTIONS

1. Lightly dust a work surface with flour and roll out the pie dough. Invert a 10-in. plate on top of the pie dough and use the plate as a template to cut around the dough's edges to make a pie shell. Discard the rest of the dough and lay the formed dough into a 9-in. pie pan, easing the dough into the bottom so that it fits snugly against all edges.

2. Fold the edges of the dough under itself so that the folded edges sit above the rim of the pie pan. Crimp the edges of the pie dough to form a decorative edge.

3. Place the pecans in the pie shell. Combine the eggs, corn syrup, brown sugar, melted butter, vanilla, and salt in a small mixing bowl and whisk until smooth. Then, pour the egg mixture over the nuts in the pie shell.

4. Slide the Pizza Rack into Shelf Position 5. Place the pie pan on the Pizza Rack. Select the Bake setting. Set the cooking temperature to 300° F/149° C and set the cooking time to 35 mins. Press the Start Button to begin the cooking cycle. Cook the pie until the crust is golden brown and the pie is just set.

5. Let the pie cool for at least 50 mins. before serving. Serve with the vanilla ice cream if desired.

INGREDIENTS

all-purpose flour, for dusting

1 store-bought or homemade prepared pie dough, room temperature

1 ½ cups chopped pecans

4 large eggs

1 ⅓ cups light corn syrup

⅔ cup light brown sugar

2 tbsp. unsalted butter, melted

1 ¼ tsp. vanilla extract

½ tsp. salt

vanilla ice cream, for serving (optional)

Sweet Potato Pie

INGREDIENTS

all-purpose flour, for dusting

1 9-in. store-bought or homemade prepared pie dough, room temperature

1 ⅓ cups cooked & mashed sweet potato

4 large eggs

½ cup heavy cream

¼ cup maple syrup

2 tbsp. light brown sugar

2 tbsp. melted butter

1 ½ tsp. vanilla extract

¾ tsp. salt

1 tsp. ground cinnamon

¼ tsp. ground nutmeg

sweetened whipped cream, for serving (optional)

DIRECTIONS

1. Lightly dust a work surface with flour and roll out the pie dough. Invert a 10-in. plate on top of the pie dough and use the plate as a template to cut around the dough's edges to make a pie shell. Discard the rest of the dough and lay the formed dough into a 9-in. pie pan, easing the dough into the bottom so that it fits snugly against all edges.

2. Fold the edges of the dough under itself so that the folded edges sit above the rim of the pie pan. Crimp the edges of the pie dough to form a decorative edge.

3. Combine the sweet potato, eggs, cream, maple syrup, brown sugar, butter, vanilla, salt, cinnamon, and nutmeg and in a bowl whisk well. Pour the sweet potato batter into the pie shell.

4. Slide the Pizza Rack into Shelf Position 5. Place the pie pan on the Pizza Rack. Select the Bake setting. Set the cooking temperature to 300° F/149° C and set the cooking time to 35 mins. Press the Start Button to begin the cooking cycle. Cook the pie until the crust is golden brown and the pie is just set.

5. Let the pie cool for at least 50 mins. before serving. Serve with the whipped cream if desired.

Peanut Butter & Chocolate Chip Cookies

MAKES 12 COOKIES

DIRECTIONS

1. Combine the peanut butter, sugar, egg, and vanilla in a mixing bowl and stir until thoroughly combined. Then, stir in the chocolate chips.

2. Use a spoon or a small scoop to divide the dough into 12 portions and roll each portion into a ball. Then, use a fork dipped in water to press downward on each ball to make crosshatch marks and flatten each ball into a cookie.

3. Select the Bake setting (325° F/165° C). Set the cooking time to 10 mins. Press the Start Button and let the Power AirFryer 360 preheat.

4. While the Power AirFryer 360 heats up, line the Baking Pan and Crisper Tray with parchment paper. Place six cookies on the Baking Pan and six cookies on the Crisper Tray.

5. Once the Power AirFryer 360 has preheated, Slide the Crisper Tray into Shelf Position 2. Slide the Pizza Rack into Shelf Position 1. Place the Baking Pan on top of the Pizza Rack. Cook until the cookies are lightly golden on top.

INGREDIENTS

1 cup creamy peanut butter

1 cup granulated sugar

1 large egg, whisked

1 tsp. vanilla extract

½ cup semisweet chocolate chips

Mixed Berry Crisp

DIRECTIONS

1. Combine the flour, oats, light brown sugar, and salt in a bowl and stir. Use a pastry blender or fork to work the butter into the flour until the crust reaches a uniform crumbly consistency to make the topping. Transfer the bowl to the freezer.

2. Toss the frozen berries and peaches with the sugar, lemon juice, and cornstarch in a separate bowl. Pour the mixture into a 1 ½-qt. casserole dish.

3. Slide the Pizza Rack into Shelf Position 6. Place the casserole dish on the Pizza Rack.

4. Select the Bake setting (325° F/165° C for 30 mins.). Press the Start Button to begin the cooking cycle. Halfway through the cooking time (15 mins.), stir the fruit gently.

5. When the cooking time is complete, top the fruit with the topping from the freezer.

6. Return the casserole dish to the Power AirFryer 360. Select the Airfry setting (400° F/205° C). Set the cooking time to 6 mins. Press the Start Button to begin the cooking cycle.

7. When the cooking time is complete, remove the casserole dish from the Power AirFryer 360. Let the crisp cool for 1 hr. before serving.

INGREDIENTS

⅓ cup flour

¼ cup rolled oats

¼ cup light brown sugar

¼ tsp. salt

¼ cup unsalted butter

1 lb frozen whole mixed berries

8 oz sliced peaches, frozen

½ cup sugar

2 tbsp. fresh lemon juice

2 ½ tbsp. cornstarch

Creole Bread Pudding

with Bourbon Sauce

INGREDIENTS

2 large eggs

⅔ cup whole milk

⅔ cup heavy cream

½ cup light brown sugar

2 tsp. vanilla extract

1 tsp. ground cinnamon

¼ tsp. ground nutmeg

¼ tsp. kosher salt

¼ cup plus 1 tbsp. unsalted butter, softened, divided

¼ cup chopped pecans

3 cups day-old bread, cut into ½-in. cubes

2 tbsp. raisins

Bourbon Sauce

1 cup whole milk

¼ cup heavy cream

¼ cup sugar

1 tbsp. plus 1 tsp. cornstarch

1 tbsp. plus 1 tsp. bourbon

1 pinch salt

DIRECTIONS

1. Combine the eggs, milk, cream, brown sugar, vanilla, cinnamon, nutmeg, and kosher salt in a bowl and whisk together. Reserve the egg mixture.

2. Place a small sauté pan on the stove top. Melt ¼ cup butter over medium heat. Add the pecans and toast for 2–3 mins. Then, remove the pan from the heat.

3. Add the bread and raisins to a mixing bowl. Add the egg mixture and the pecan mixture to the bread and stir to combine. Set aside for 30 mins.

4. Butter a 1 ½-qt.casserole dish with the rest of the butter and then add the bread pudding mixture.

5. Slide the Pizza Rack into Shelf Position 5. Place the casserole dish on the Pizza Rack.

6. Select the Bake setting (325° F/165° C for 30 mins.). Press the Start Button to begin the cooking cycle.

7. When the cooking time is complete, transfer the casserole dish to a wire rack and let cool for at least 30 mins.

8. While the bread pudding cools, make the sauce: Place a small saucepot on the stove top. Bring the milk, cream, and sugar to a simmer.

9. Combine the cornstarch and bourbon in a small bowl. Stir the bourbon mixture into the simmering cream and whisk until thickened. Then, stir in the salt.

10. Serve the bread pudding with the bourbon sauce.

Lemon Poppy Seed Cake

SERVES 6–8

DIRECTIONS

1. Combine the coconut milk, eggs, and vanilla in a medium-size bowl and whisk well to combine.

2. Combine the flour, sugar, baking soda, salt, poppy seeds, and lemon zest in a separate bowl and whisk well to combine.

3. Add the butter and half of the coconut mixture to the dry ingredients and use an electric mixer to mix the ingredients on low speed. Once the ingredients are mixed, increase the speed to medium-high and beat for 1 min.

4. Scrape down the sides of the bowl and gradually add the rest of the coconut milk mixture in two batches, beating for at least 25 secs. after each addition.

5. Spoon the batter into a standard-size loaf pan that has been greased/buttered.

6. Select the Bake setting (325° F/165° C). Set the cooking time to 20 mins. Press the Start Button and let the Power AirFryer 360 preheat.

7. Once the Power AirFryer 360 has preheated, Slide the Pizza Rack into Shelf Position 5. Place the loaf pan on the Pizza Rack.

8. Once the cooking time is complete, remove the loaf pan from the Power AirFryer 360 and let the cakes cool before serving.

INGREDIENTS

3 tbsp. coconut milk

3 large eggs

2 tsp. vanilla extract

1 ½ cups sifted cake flour

¾ cup sugar

¾ tsp. baking soda

¼ tsp. fine salt

3 tbsp. poppy seeds

1 tbsp. lemon zest

12 tbsp. unsalted butter, softened

Blueberry Pie

DIRECTIONS

1. Place a small saucepan on the stove top. Add the blueberries, sugar, lemon zest, and mace. Cook over medium heat while stirring until the sugar has dissolved and the mixture begins to look soupy (about 5 mins.).

2. Combine the cornstarch and water in a small bowl and whisk together. Pour the mixture into the saucepan with the blueberries and cook while stirring until the mixture begins to thicken. Once the mixture has thickened, remove the saucepan from the heat and let the mixture cool.

3. Select the Bake setting. Set the cooking temperature to 310° F/154° C and set the cooking time to 45 mins. Press the Start Button and let the Power AirFryer 360 preheat.

4. Roll out the dough sheets on a lightly floured surface until they are ⅛ in. thick. Place a pie pan on the dough and cut a round ¾ in. larger than the pie pan from one of the sheets. Press the dough into the pan and trim any excess dough from around the sides. Then, add the filling.

5. Make a lattice top by cutting the second sheet of dough into eight 1-in. pieces and weave the dough to form the lattice. Transfer the lattice to the top of the pie.

6. Once the Power AirFryer 360 has preheated, slide the Pizza Rack into Shelf Position 5. Place the pie pan on the Pizza Rack. Cook until the crust is golden brown.

7. Let the pie rest for about 2 hrs. before serving.

INGREDIENTS

5 cups blueberries

1 ¼ cups granulated sugar

½ tsp. lemon zest

1 pinch mace

2 ½ tbsp. cornstarch

3 tbsp. water

¾ tsp. vanilla extract

2 sheets store-bought pie dough

Index